THE
BUILDINGS
THAT
REVOLUTIONIZED
ARCHITECTURE

THE BUILDINGS THAT REVOLUTIONIZED ARCHITECTURE

FLORIAN HEINE AND ISABEL KUHL

PRESTEL

Munich · London · New York

CONTENTS

FOREWORD

Architecture is often referred to as the 'mother of all art' in that it brings together the other arts under its roof. This may well be the case, but architecture is different in that it must also meet very functional and practical demands that do not apply to the other arts. Jacques Herzog, who collaborated on the construction of the Beijing National Stadium, had the following to say in 2004 on the subject of art and architecture: 'Architecture is architecture, and art is art. Architecture as art is unbearable.'

In keeping with this dictum, the 100 works of architecture introduced here are pure architecture, though they do also meet the highest artistic standards. Covering four millennia, located all over the globe and shaped by a wide variety of influences, they form an overview of how architecture has developed over time. Architecture has always had the same fundamental importance throughout the course of history, and has played a similar role across all the continents.

Everyday 'functional architecture' is only of minor significance in the 'art history' of architecture, and is only rarely discussed. The history of architecture is generally concerned with the high-profile projects that, over the centuries, have often been constructed to great acclaim, combining considerable artistic and financial effort. These include temples, churches, residences and, more recently, factories and museums, to name a few examples. Yet architecture has often had – and continues to have – a greater influence on its environment, and even on history, than its protagonists may realise at the time. St Peter's in Rome, for example, was a catalyst for the Reformation in the same way the Great Wall of China was responsible for the end of the Ming dynasty. A more recent example is the Guggenheim Museum in Bilbao and the tremendously positive effect it has always had on the economy of the entire region.

Architects are always also innovators, who constantly come up with new possibilities, techniques and materials with which to execute their ideas. Examples include the master builders of the Gothic period: Filippo Brunelleschi when he constructed the dome for the cathedral in Florence, Thomas Pritchard, who built the first iron bridge, Walter Gropius, whose small-scale Fagus factory fired the starting shot for great innovation, and Shigeru Ban, who discovered that cardboard could be used for architecture. The importance of the relationship between the person commissioning the work and the architect should not be underestimated, however. Rulers, church dignitaries and the bosses of companies have often shown great foresight and courage in their decisions to commission one particular architect or another. The fact that part of their motivation is often rooted in the desire to demonstrate power and influence, for which architects have developed a language, is probably inevitable. As Shigeru Ban has said, 'We are supposed to make power and money visible through monumental architecture.'

Whatever the motives for individual commissions may have been, master builders, engineers and architects have continuously developed architecture over the course of the centuries. The 100 works of architecture presented in this book provide an overview of that development throughout the world. It is, sadly, not possible for a book to do justice to the character and effect of a building in just a few photographs. The aim of *The Buildings That Revolutionized Architecture* is therefore also to serve as an inspiration and invitation to visit one or other of the buildings in person in order to fully experience the diversity of architecture at close range.

Florian Heine

THE PYRAMIDS OF GIZA, CIRCA 2620–2500 BC

1

PYRAMIDS OF GIZA

Mark Twain's memory of climbing the Great Pyramid of Cheops was not a pleasant one. The effect of the gigantic structure on the west bank of the Nile changed as the traveller approached it. The 'fairy vision' that he had seen from afar eventually became 'a corrugated, unsightly mountain of stone'.

No doubt the tiring ascent greatly contributed to this damning judgement, as the largest architectural structure of the ancient world must have been impressive even in its guise as a mountain of stone: the most imposing of the Egyptian pyramids, the burial site of Pharaoh Cheops is the last of the Seven Wonders of the Ancient World still in existence. It was built around the middle of the third millennium BC in Giza, just a few kilometres south-west of Cairo. To date, more than 80 pyramids have been discovered along the Nile valley, an entire city of the dead that is visible from afar in the flat landscape on the edge of the Libyan Desert. Although Cheops commissioned the biggest of the royal burial sites, the neighbouring pyramids of his son Chephren and of Chephren's son Myke-rinos are only marginally smaller. The queens were buried in three smaller pyramids, and they are surrounded by hundreds of other graves and temples, making the pyramid fields an enormous graveyard.

Thousands of labourers worked for almost 30 years on the construction of the first pyramid alone, the burial site of Cheops. They layered an unimaginable 2.5 million stones on top of one another. Thousands of stonemasons were in charge of supplying blocks of limestone, basalt and granite from quarries. The total weight of the Great Pyramid of Cheops is estimated at more than six million tonnes. If one counts servants and haulers, between 20,000 and 25,000 people – approximately one per cent of the total population of Egypt – are thought to have been employed in the construction of the Great Pyramid of Cheops. The architects included experts in mathemat-ics, who appear to have had no trouble calculating the precise volumes and right angles. Starting from a square ground plan, the pyramids rise as triangles that intersect at the tip. The smooth surfaces converge without a step despite the fact that the edges measure more than 230 metres. The entrance to the pyramid lay in the north, from which a low passageway sloped downwards. The burial chamber constitutes the centre of the body of the building, in which the stone sarcophagus containing the embalmed body of the pharaoh was laid to rest. The Egyptians were convinced that the dead pharaoh lived for all eternity in his pyramid, so that it was essential to supply and protect him for all eternity. Heavy stones protected the burial chamber from intruders in search of precious burial furnishings, and the circulation of fresh air was ensured. Despite all precautions, the burial chamber was looted, possibly even during the age of the pharaohs. Its reputation as a Wonder of the World remains undiminished, however.

2

GREAT TEMPLE, ABU SIMBEL

It must have been an astonishing sight when Jean Louis Burckhardt (1784–1817) saw the great stone head of Ramesses II jutting out of a sand dune in 1813. Shortly beforehand, the Swiss explorer of the Orient had been the first European to see Petra, a city hewn from rock. He cannot have guessed what he had just discovered on the border to Sudan: the temples of Pharaoh Ramesses II (circa 1303–1213 BC) and his principal wife, Nefertari, which were built on the occasion of the 30th anniversary of his accession to the throne.

The pharaoh's great temple was cut 63 metres into the rock between 1290 and 1260 BC. Two pairs of colossal seated statues representing the deified pharaoh (each measuring 22 metres in height) can be seen along the façade, which is 33 metres high and 35 metres wide. A hypostyle hall, eight metres in height and painted in colour, features statues and reliefs depicting military scenes of the conquest of Nubia. It is followed by a chamber that represents the holy centre of the temple. Here, Ramesses is represented in the midst of the divine trinity. Burckhardt saw none of this because the excavations did not begin until 1817, under the Italian Giovanni Battista Belzoni (1778–1823), and were not (for the most part) completed until 1909. Early photographs from circa 1850 show the enormous stone heads still deeply buried in the sand.

Even before Ramesses II ordered the temple to be built, this was the site of two sacred grottoes dedicated to the local gods of the vanquished Nubians. The construction of the temples must therefore also be understood as a symbol of the worldly and religious submission of the Nubians to the Egyptian kingdom: as a symbol of power. They were also an 'offshoot' of the main royal palace in Thebes.

The temple complex gained particular fame and importance – in addition to its significance as evidence of the former vastness of the Egyptian kingdom – when the Aswan Dam was planned and the temple complex threatened to be submerged in Lake Nasser. This gave rise to the extraordinary idea of moving the temples. An international consortium was founded and what must have been the most unusual archaeological task of its time began in November 1963. First the structures were hardened using 33 tonnes of epoxy resin, and then they were sawn into 1,036 blocks weighing between seven and 30 tonnes each. The temples were dismantled bit by bit, and reassembled 180 metres to the north-west and 65 metres higher up. Particular attention was paid to the temple's precise alignment with the sun because the sun illuminates the innermost section of the Great Temple on the spring and autumn equinox.

As these particular temples are hewn into the rock, the rock, too, had to be moved. The interior of the Great Temple is supported by a steel dome 140 metres high. It is no longer visible for it has been covered by sand, stones and 1,112 pieces of rock from the original surroundings. The procedure was not completed until September 1968. The project, which cost some 80 million US dollars and was financed by more than 50 states, was one of the main reasons for the foundation of the UNESCO World Heritage Convention of 1972 and the establishment of the World Cultural Heritage List. The temple complex of Abu Simbel is evidence of both the brilliance of the ancient Egyptians and the engineering skill of the 20th century. It also shows what can be achieved by a united world community to preserve the world's heritage. The temple complex itself was not included in the list until 1979.

'OH YE LABOURERS, SELECTED, STRONG, DILIGENT OF HAND, WHO ERECT ALL NUMBER OF MONUMENTS FOR ME, EXPERIENCED AT WORKING WITH PRECIOUS STONES, RECOGNISING TYPES OF GRANITE AND FAMILIAR WITH SANDSTONE. OH YE DILIGENT AND INDUSTRIOUS BUILDERS OF MONUMENTS! I SHALL LIVE AS LONG AS THEY!'

Homage of Ramesses II to his workers

THE GREAT TEMPLE, ABU SIMBEL, 1290–1260 BC

3

THE GREAT WALL OF CHINA

The Great Wall of China is not one, unified structure but the sum of many parts built over the course of two thousand years. Until recently, estimates of its length had ranged from 4,000 to 6,500 kilometres and beyond. The wall features approximately 25,000 towers, and its hundreds of elements are spread out across China. Impressive as these numbers are, the wall cannot in fact be seen from space with the naked eye.

The Chinese name for the Great Wall is 'The Long Wall of 10,000 Li'. With one *li* equal to 575.5 metres, this corresponds to an overall length of 5,755 kilometres, which comes close to several estimates. In Chinese, however, the figure 10,000 has the additional meaning of 'an infinite number' or 'unimaginably long', both of which are suitable descriptions of the wall. The part that is often referred to as the Great Wall was constructed during the Ming dynasty (1368 to 1644), whereas the oldest section appears to have been built as long ago as 214 BC by the first emperor of China, Qin Shihuangdi, as protection against the peoples of the north. Some researchers believe that construction began as far back as the 7th century BC. These very old sections of the wall are more like mounds of earth that were shored up with clay and natural stone. The wall was continually expanded over the centuries. The section of wall dating to the Ming dynasty was built starting in 1493, or 1555 at the latest. Its aim was both to provide protection against the Mongols and to control trade. It extends from the west part, the Jade Gate, over mountains, rivers and lakes, and ends in the east at the Dragon's Head, jutting out into the sea at Shanhaiguan. Only about a twelfth of the wall – some 500 kilometres of the 6,000 kilometres or so that make up the wall are well preserved, however. The rest has fallen into disrepair or was dismantled for building materials over the course of centuries. During its extended construction period the wall was built to a thickness of six to ten metres and up to 16 metres in height. One of the 25,000 towers was erected every couple of hundred metres. They were effective both as fortifications and for signalling.

In 2012 China published the results of a new archaeological survey of the Great Wall and declared it to be considerably longer than previously thought, extending 21,196.18 kilometres across 15 provinces. The measuring, involving two thousand researchers and technicians, had taken four years to complete. How long the wall really is, and which of its many sections should be included in the measurements, is obviously a matter of opinion. But this is not the most important issue. The wall is clearly the world's largest man-made structure, and its history ended in 1644 with the fall of the Ming dynasty, ushered in by the Manchu conquest of China in the east. Originally built to ward off invasion, the wall had in fact long been a symbol of an isolationist view of the world with which China, certain of its own greatness, rejected engagement with the rest of the world.

For the Chinese themselves, the Great Wall did not begin to regain significance until after Mao's Cultural Revolution (1966–76), when it came to be seen as an ideal symbol of national identity – and continues to be so regarded.

'A WALL FOUR HUNDRED MILES LONG WAS ERECTED BY THE KING
BETWEEN THE MOUNTAIN CRESTS TO DEFEND AGAINST THE INVASIONS
OF THE TATARS IN THIS REGION.'

From Abraham Ortelius, *Atlas Theatrum Orbis Terrarum*, 1584, including the first Western map of China

THE GREAT WALL OF CHINA, BEGUN IN 214 BC

THE PARTHENON, ATHENS, DEDICATED IN 438 BC

4

PARTHENON, ATHENS

It took five tonnes of silver to build the central temple on the Acropolis. The powerful city of Athens erected a magnificent monument to its patron goddess: a vast temple of white marble, decorated inside and out with sculptures, was created within the space of just 15 years.

During the 5th century BC, Athens developed into one of the largest city-states in ancient Greece. Under the leadership of Pericles the city prospered: it became an important trading centre that underlined its power through a large navy, and it transformed itself into a democracy. This golden age was also reflected in the city architecture. On the Acropolis, the 'Castle Hill', Pericles was instrumental in the rebuilding of the temples destroyed during the war against the Persians, especially the Parthenon. Work began in 447 BC under the architect Iktinos: a hall of monumental columns, each of them more than ten metres in height, was constructed on an area measuring about 30 metres by 70 metres. Eight columns stand on the east and west fronts, and 17 on each of the long sides. These proportions determine the entire building. A horizontal beam rests on the columns, supporting a triangular gable on each of the two fronts.

The imposing marble temple was dedicated to the tutelary goddess of the city, Athena. Her statue, ten metres tall, stood in the cella, the innermost sanctuary of the temple. Apart from the wooden core, the figure was primarily of gold – more than 1,000 kilograms all told – and ivory, and she was decorated with precious stones. These valuable materials also formed part of the city treasury of Athens as well as the treasury of the Attic Naval Alliance, which the Greeks had founded in order to repulse the Persians. Athens levied some 11 tonnes of silver every year from its allies.

In building the Parthenon, the city-state emphasised its political significance. The sculpture that formed part of the architecture was correspondingly elaborate: Pericles commissioned the sculptor Phidias, who was famous even during his own lifetime, to create the pictorial decoration of the temple. The reliefs and sculptures showed scenes from historical battles and sieges, processions and parades full of pomp. Until well into the 17th century the temple resisted the ravages of time, but then a Venetian cannonball hit the gunpowder magazine that was stored there and badly damaged the building. Only parts of the sculptural ornamentation have survived, and for a long time they have not been in their original location: in around 1800, the British ambassador Lord Elgin had large sections removed and sold them to a purchaser in London. The so-called Elgin Marbles can now be admired in the British Museum; the debate surrounding their return to Athens continues. Despite all the ravages, the Parthenon is one of the most famous monuments of ancient Greece.

THE GREEK TEMPLES OF ANTIQUITY usually stood on a base with a rectangular ground plan. Their core was an elongated inner space, the cella, which was surrounded by a columned arcade. In the cella stood the cult image – in the case of the Parthenon, a monumental statue of Athena. Heavy cross-beams lay on the tapered columns of this round peripteral temple: horizontal building elements like load-bearing beams, friezes and lintels. The aim was to arrive at a harmonious relationship between vertical and horizontal lines. Architectural ornaments, including sculptures and relief friezes, adorned the otherwise simple buildings; the temples and their sculptural decoration were often also painted.

'THE PEOPLE OF EPIDAURUS HAVE A THEATRE IN THE SANCTUARY
THAT IS, IN MY OPINION, PARTICULARLY WORTH SEEING.'

Pausanias

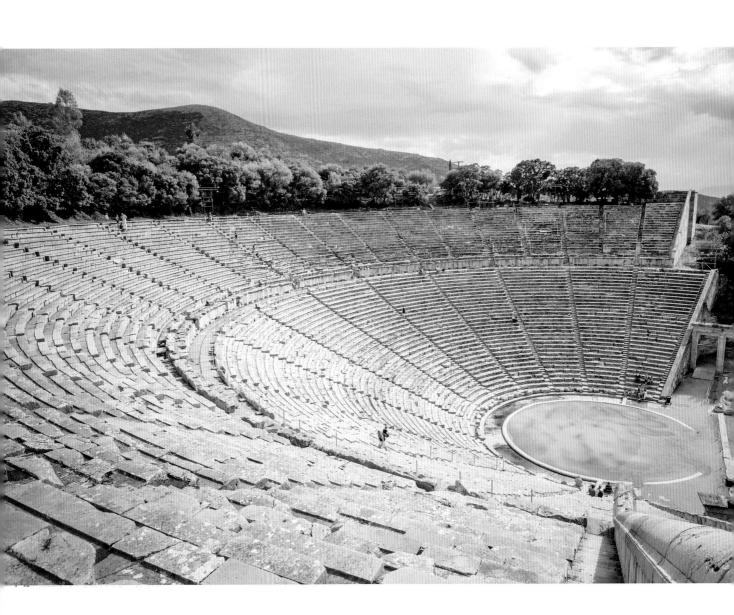

THE THEATRE OF EPIDAURUS, CIRCA 330 BC

5

THEATRE OF EPIDAURUS

Thus wrote the Greek traveller and geographer Pausanias (flourished circa AD 143–176) in his ***Description of Greece***. And the theatre continues to be worth a visit because it is the most well preserved of classical Greek theatres.

The theatre was, however, just one part of the sanctuary of Asclepius, which was built here, in the mythical birthplace of the god of healing, from the 4th century BC. Epidaurus was a centre of pilgrimage and healing, in other words, something like a sacred sanatorium comparable with Lourdes and Fatima. The Greek geographer and historian Strabo (circa 63 BC–circa AD 23) wrote in his *Geography*: 'This city, too, is important, in particular because of the fame of Asclepius, who is believed to cure all sorts of diseases and whose temple is always filled with the sick.' In addition to the temples and sanatorium areas, there was a stadium and a theatre. This is because Asclepius's art of healing included not only the right diet, baths, medicinal plants and surgery, but also drama. The tragedies – and probably also comedies – aimed to touch people and develop their sense of empathy in order to cleanse their souls.

Most of the buildings of Epidaurus fell victim to the earthquakes of AD 522 and 551. Only the theatre has survived the passage of time and is the largest extant ancient Greek theatre. Pausanias names Polyclitus the Younger as the architect, though this remains unconfirmed. The theatre was built into a north-facing rock at Epidaurus in circa 330 BC, and had a capacity of 6,500 spectators. The 'theatron' (viewing area) consisted of 34 rows arranged around the circular 'orchestra' (performance area for the choir) in 12 wedge-shaped segments divided by the staircases. Only the outline of the 'skene' (two-storey stage building) and of the 'proskenion' remain today. The latter was the actual elevated performance area (measuring 22 by 2.17 metres) and it stood before a backdrop of a hall with 14 ionic half-columns. This could be used to stage 'special effects', including flying gods and the like, and various panels could be inserted between the columns as a stage set.

The theatre did not exist in its present state until the second phase of construction in the first half of the 2nd century. It seems audience numbers were so high that another 21 rows of seats were added. The theatre could now seat 14,000 people. This theatre is remarkable not only for its size, but also for its extraordinarily good acoustics. Even a whisper in the circular orchestra is clearly audible in the back row at the top, at a distance of approximately 60 metres. There are several reasons for this, including the arrangement of the seats: those built in the second construction phase in particular rise steeply and are concave. Secondly, it is clear that earthenware dishes were incorporated into the front rows as resonating bodies. Most importantly, perhaps, the surfaces of the rows of seats are not entirely smooth; they are rough, as is the case in modern recording studios. As a result, sounds have only short reverberations, which therefore do not overlap with their own echoes as they travel all the way to the back rows of seats.

The Asclepius sanctuary was destroyed by the Goths in AD 267, and later rebuilt. In AD 426 it was finally shut down by the Christian Emperor Theodosius II. Nowadays it is used as a performance space for classical theatre once again.

'IN THE RED SANDSTONE, OF WHICH THE ENTIRE VALLEY IS MADE,
LIE ROUGHLY TWO HUNDRED AND FIFTY GRAVES, ENTIRELY HEWN
FROM THE ROCK ... THESE INCLUDE A MAUSOLEUM IN THE
SHAPE OF A TEMPLE, WHICH IS OF COLOSSAL DIMENSIONS
AND THIS, TOO, IS HEWN FROM THE ROCK ...'

Jean Louis Burckhardt

PETRA, JORDAN, 1ST CENTURY BC (?)

6

PETRA, JORDAN

The 'treasury of the pharaoh' has the most famous façade in all of Petra, the ancient city carved from rock. The American director Steven Spielberg used it as a façade behind which Indiana Jones suspected the Holy Grail. Researchers, as well as film-makers, continue to be enraptured by the imposing structure of reddish sandstone.

The Siq provides the only direct access to the ancient settlement in the desert of Jordan. More than one kilometre long, this narrow ravine between high cliffs leads to the city. Petra was an important base for the Nabataeans. The desert people established permanent settlements some two thousand years ago, and engaged in trade along the Incense Route in the north of the Arabian Peninsula. Petra was the junction of two roads through the desert, benefiting from the irrigation skills of the Nabataeans. A water conduit hewn into the rock kept the city supplied with water, which was stored in basins and tanks for the dry season. The natural fortress thus became an oasis in the desert, and its fortunes rose rapidly. Caravans stopped here, and the trading post between the cliffs became an economic and political centre. The upswing was accompanied by great building projects, all of which were realised using the local sandstone, which has a red sheen. The city's name means 'rock'.

The structures carved out of the rock include an entire theatre that accommodated around 8,000 spectators, as well as temples and shopping arcades along what was the main street. Since the ruins of the Nabataean city were discovered by the Swiss explorer of the Orient Jean Louis Burckhardt, archaeologists have examined only a small fragment of the area covered by the city. In the autumn of 1812 he wrote an enthusiastic letter about his journey to 'a place that […] no other European traveller has ever visited', and described the countless graves in the Greek and Egyptian style. The monumental scale of the burial structures, many of which are accessible via rock steps, is in itself impressive. Their façades frequently span two storeys, and they often feature columns and gables, parapets and arches, or they are embellished with rich sculptural details that have been carved out of the smooth surface of the rock. Some of the grave façades measuring several metres in height were even painted in a variety of colours. The most famous façade of the desert city lies on a big square surrounded by cliffs. The two-storey front of the 'treasury', which is thought also to have been a temple or a burial structure, rises to a height of almost 40 metres. The middle four of the six columns on the ground floor are surmounted by a pediment, and a pavilion-like circular structure is embedded between the sides of a broken pediment. Behind the magnificent façade lies a closed burial chamber that is thought to have housed stone sarcophagi. However, Indiana Jones remains the only archaeologist to date to have discovered the precise location of the door leading to the Guardians of the Holy Grail.

7

COLOSSEUM, ROME

Mark Twain called the Colosseum the 'monarch of all European ruins'. When the American writer visited the Roman amphitheatre, its history already spanned about 1,800 years. Although faded and crumbled, its monumental dimensions were impressive: in ancient Rome, the various tiers of seating accommodated as many as 70,000 spectators, who came to witness the battles between fearless gladiators and wild animals.

The gigantic amphitheatre on the edge of the ancient city centre is the most famous architectural structure of the reign of Emperor Vespasian, who was nothing if not imaginative when it came to methods for collecting the funds necessary for his building projects. One day, while explaining his newest source of money to his son, he used the now famous expression 'Money does not stink!' – and promptly instituted a latrine tax. Thanks to innovative financial measures such as these, the Colosseum was built in record time: work began in the year AD 72 and was completed just eight years later. Built on an oval ground plan, the outermost ring of the amphitheatre is almost 50 metres high. And the arena itself covers an area measuring approximately 80 by 50 metres. The façade is decorated with rows of arches that vary from one storey to the next.

On the ground floor, 80 arches open onto steps inside. Four of the entrances on the main axes of the theatre were reserved for the exclusive use of high-ranking visitors. The common people entered the theatre through the remaining entrances. The four storeys of the building were divided into tiers and blocks, which the visitors accessed through a system of meticulously planned paths and entrances. Sophisticated logistical systems guaranteed that the spectacles ran smoothly, and yet access was free. The seating was rigidly regulated, however, with a strict separation according to origins, status and occupation. The first row behind the emperor's box, for example, was reserved for senators, and women had to make do with galleries located at the back.

The Colosseum remained an arena for popular spectacles until the 5th century: gladiatorial battles and animal hunts were regularly held for large audiences, and even sea battles were staged here, for which the enormous arena was flooded. Then Rome and its Colosseum fell silent. The building, which had in the meantime become a ruin, was forgotten until the Renaissance, when the popes needed building materials for their colossal architectural projects. The Colosseum certainly provided an abundant supply: approximately 100,000 cubic metres of travertine, as well as the marble used to cover the lower rows of seats, not to mention around 300 tonnes of iron, for the individual stone blocks were connected by metal pins, and these, too, were a building material popular with later generations. Despite its career as a quarry, and in defiance of earthquakes and fires, about two-fifths of the façade are still in place today. And what is left has impressed visitors to Rome since long before Mark Twain made his journey.

'EVERYBODY KNOWS THE PICTURE OF THE COLISEUM;
EVERYBODY RECOGNIZES AT ONCE THAT "LOOPED AND
WINDOWED" BANDBOX WITH A SIDE BITTEN OUT.'

Mark Twain

THE COLOSSEUM, ROME, AD 72–80

8

PANTHEON, ROME

The inscription emblazoned on the gable of the best-preserved building of Roman antiquity is misleading. It was not built by Marcus Agrippa; it was in fact Emperor Hadrian who had this unusual edifice erected between AD 118 and 125, in other words, almost a century after Agrippa's earlier building.

As the name indicates, the Pantheon was a temple for all the Roman gods. Following its rededication by Pope Boniface IV in 609 as Santa Maria ad Martyres, it became a Christian church and was thus saved from major damage by the barbarians, or the Romans themselves who needed building materials. One famous exception was Pope Urban VIII Barberini, who in 1632 had the bronze cladding of the portico removed and the 200 tonnes of bronze cast into 80 cannons for the Castello Sant'Angelo; the rest he gave to Gian Lorenzo Bernini for his *baldacchino* in St Peter's Basilica. This act was the source of the Romans' comment regarding the destruction of Rome: 'The Barberini have done what the barbarians failed to do.'

In contrast to Greek temple architecture, in which the interior was taboo for the common people, the Pantheon was built precisely for them. An essential difference between Greek and Roman religious architecture is that whereas the Greeks were interested above all in a perfect exterior, for the Romans, it was the interior space that mattered most. And the Pantheon remains one of the most fascinating interiors in the history of architecture. Visitors cross the triple-naved portico with its 16 massive Corinthian pillars and pass through the six-metre-high bronze door into a windowless interior lit only by an oculus nine metres in diameter in the ceiling. Contrary to what one would expect in view of the cylindrical external structure, the proportions here are well balanced. The arch of the rotunda, which begins exactly halfway up, sits on the cylindrical base and tapers towards the top with five coffered rings. The interior thus consists of a cylinder positioned on top of a hemispherical dome. The interior encloses an imaginary sphere with a diameter of 43.2 metres. The walls are subdivided by alternate rectangular and semicircular niches. Until the 20th century the Pantheon was the world's largest domed structure. The Roman master builders used an early form of cement in which the mortar was mixed with aggregate stones and bricks, as well as volcanic rock. This permitted a lighter and more flexible form of construction that proved an advantage in the construction of the rotunda because the walls of the lower section, which were more than six metres thick, became progressively thinner and lighter towards the top. The shearing forces of the arch were diverted into the walls and the buttresses surrounding the building.

If, in our mind's eye, we replace the Christian paintings and statues with Roman ones, we can imagine ourselves in ancient Rome. In fact the interior of the Pantheon has remained more or less unchanged for the past almost two thousand years. What has changed, though, is the piazza surrounding the Pantheon, because the ground level has risen across the centuries. When it was built, visitors had to climb five steps to reach the portico. Accordingly, the cylindrical main structure looked more massive; today it appears somewhat depressed.

The Pantheon frequently served as inspiration for later architects like Bramante and Michelangelo, whose concept for St Peter's Basilica (see page 102) was to mount the Pantheon on top of the Basilica of Maxentius.

'SIMPLE, ERECT, SEVERE, AUSTERE, SUBLIME –
... SPARED AND BLEST BY TIME; / LOOKING TRANQUILLITY, WHILE FALLS
OR NODS / ARCH, EMPIRE, EACH THING ROUND THEE,
AND MAN PLODS / HIS WAY THROUGH THORNS TO ASHES – GLORIOUS DOME! /
... SANCTUARY AND HOME / OF ART AND PIETY – PANTHEON! –
PRIDE OF ROME!'

George Gordon, Lord Byron

THE PANTHEON, ROME, CIRCA AD 118–25

The Pantheon was elevated above the level of the square at the time of its construction and was accessible via five steps. The building's relatively unspectacular exterior and its proportions do not hint at its extraordinary interior.

'AND IT ABOUNDS EXCEEDINGLY IN SUNLIGHT AND IN
THE REFLECTION OF THE SUN'S RAYS FROM THE MARBLE.
INDEED ONE MIGHT SAY THAT ITS INTERIOR IS NOT ILLUMINATED FROM
WITHOUT BY THE SUN, BUT THAT THE RADIANCE COMES INTO BEING WITHIN
IT, SUCH AN ABUNDANCE OF LIGHT BATHES THIS SHRINE.'

Procopius, *On the Buildings* (of Justinian), mid-6th century

THE HAGIA SOPHIA, ISTANBUL, 532–37

9

HAGIA SOPHIA, ISTANBUL

The American writer Mark Twain did not have a good word to say about it: 'St. Sophia is a colossal church, thirteen or fourteen hundred years old, and unsightly enough to be very, very much older.' During an extended journey as a travel journalist, the picture he drew of the sights around the Mediterranean was sometimes quite dismal.

Nonetheless, the vast dome of the Church of the Holy Wisdom in the heart of Istanbul compelled him to admit to admiration: it was finer than that of St Peter's in Rome, but 'its dirt is much more wonderful than its dome, though they never mention it.' Unlike Twain, earlier visitors to the building had tended to extol it in extravagant praises. The historian Procopius, for example, had reported its 'indescribable beauty' during the 6th century. When it was built, the church, located in the cultural and trading centre of Constantinople – present-day Istanbul – was by far the biggest church in Christendom. During the Middle Ages, the monumental complex was included among the Seven Wonders of the Ancient World. The vast dome in particular, apparently suspended in mid-air, and also the vaulting, demand respect even of modern visitors: the main dome is almost 56 metres high and has a diameter of 31 metres. How the master builders in the 6th century succeeded in constructing it remains a mystery. We do at least know the names of the architects: Anthemius of Tralles and Isidore of Miletus. And we also know who commissioned it: Emperor Justinian I wanted to perpetuate his memory as emperor with this gargantuan building project. His church, in the capital of the Eastern Roman Empire, was completed in what may well have been the record construction time of six years, from 532 until 537. According to contemporary sources, 10,000 workers realised the enormous building, for which they used some 145 tonnes of gold. The gold was used, among other things, for the grained marble and the gold mosaics that decorated the floors and walls: the interior of the domed basilica with its columns, aisles and galleries was elaborately adorned with precious materials. But not much remains of this impression of riches and space: when the Turks conquered Constantinople in 1453, they turned the Hagia Sophia into the principal mosque of the Ottoman Empire. The furnishings were largely removed and the mosaics were covered up or plastered over because of the Islamic ban on images. And even the exterior changed its appearance: to this day the four minarets, which were added shortly afterwards, determine the impression made by the building. In 1934 the mosque was transformed into a museum. Mark Twain's derogatory description of the Hagia Sophia has not harmed its career as a magnet for visitors. Maybe, as he admitted, he just failed to understand it …

left The Hagia Sophia in Istanbul is considered to be the prototype of the *plan centré* building surmounted by a dome. Emperor Justinian ordered it to be built in just six years starting in 532. Its dome rests on massive pillars and spans more than 30 metres.

above The great early Christian church was reconsecrated as a mosque after the city had been conquered by the Ottomans. Much of the original wealth of the interior decorations has been lost. A number of mosaics and murals have been exposed again since the Hagia Sophia was turned into a museum in 1934.

SAN VITALE, RAVENNA, 526–47

10

SAN VITALE, RAVENNA

Ravenna was an important cultural centre of the Roman Empire – the little town on the Adriatic now looks like an open-air museum for early Christian art. Another golden age began when the Byzantines captured the flourishing port city in the year 540. Large buildings were commissioned, the most elaborate of which is San Vitale.

A mediaeval chronicler concluded that no church in Italy was its equal, 'neither in terms of its architecture nor in artistic and technical terms'. It was also recorded that 120 kilogrammes of gold were used in its construction, the foundation stone for which was laid in 526 by Bishop Ecclesius. The exterior of San Vitale with its reddish brick walls is fairly plain. One must enter the church to discover why it made such a profound impression on contemporaries. Even the construction type was unusual: San Vitale is built on an octagonal plan, and a high dome surmounts its centre. It is likely that this architectural form was imported from Constantinople; the Hagia Sophia (see page 26) is also executed as a *plan centré* with a dome. The central octagon in Ravenna is surrounded by an ambulatory that opens up onto the interior in high circular arches. It extends to two storeys, with galleries surmounted by half-domes in the upper storey. An elongated choir that leads to a semicircular apse is attached in the east. This part of the building in particular is an impressive example of the mosaic art of Byzantine late antiquity. The apse is carpeted with mosaics from the base to the ceiling. The many little pieces of coloured glass, semi-precious stones and gold-leaf surfaces sparkle in countless shades of colour and gold. On the wall at the end of the sanctuary Christ presides over a paradisiacal garden, surrounded by saints and angels dressed in white robes. The large mosaic sections on both sides of the windows below represent worldly rulers with their retinues, probably Emperor Justinian and his wife, Theodora, both wearing magnificent robes.

The adjacent vaulted section, too, is entirely decorated with mosaics: angels and saints populate the walls, which, along with the alcoves and ceiling vaults, are covered with architectural representations and botanical and geometrical ornaments. Scenes from the Old and New Testament are juxtaposed with one another, forming an iconographic programme that can be interpreted as the Story of Salvation.

Originally, the entire interior of the church was brightly coloured: mosaics graced the walls, ceilings and floors, and coloured panes of glass in shades of blue, purple, green and brown heightened the magnificent effect of the colours. One illustrious visitor, however, was more impressed by the basic form of the church than he was by its interior: Charlemagne drew on the design of San Vitale when building his chapel in the Palace of Aachen in circa 800.

In a **PLAN CENTRÉ** all parts of the structure are connected to the centre. The footprint of a *plan centré* might consist of a circle, an oval or a square, for example. It could also rise above a polygon, such as an octagon, or a cross with arms of equal length. The central space can open onto an ambulatory, as it does in Ravenna, and it is often surmounted with a dome. One of the oldest extant buildings constructed on a *plan centré* is the Pantheon in Rome. This design was often used for sepulchral churches and baptisteries, and this type of building was of particular significance in Byzantine architecture. During the Italian Renaissance, the architect Andrea Palladio also used a *plan centré* layout for secular buildings.

above San Vitale is richly decorated with mosaics that juxtapose scenes from the Old and New Testament. In the church's apse, Christ is enthroned between angels, accompanied by St Vitalis and Bishop Ecclesius. Ecclesius holds a model of San Vitale in his hands because he laid the foundation stone for the building.

right The church consists of an octagon crowned by a dome. This is supported by eight pillars that open onto an arcade. The central dome, too, is decorated with figural and ornamental representations.

SAN VITALE, RAVENNA, 526–47

11

HŌRYŪ-JI, NARA

Prince Shōtoku laid the foundation stone for the Hōryū-ji in the 7th century. The Japanese temple complex is the only architectural structure to survive in its entirety from the early period of Buddhist architecture. The ensemble of buildings also houses some of the oldest wooden buildings in the world.

Buddhist teachings reached Japan around the middle of the 6th century. Prince Shōtoku in particular was instrumental in their dissemination and numerous Buddhist temples were built during his reign. The Hōryū-ji, or Temple of the Flourishing Law, is one of them. The temple complex is located ten kilometres south-west of the city of Nara on the main island of the Japanese archipelago. Construction began in the year 607, using the traditional Japanese wood construction technique. The presence of the temple hall, the five-storey pagoda and the middle arch mean that the oldest wooden buildings in the world are to be found on the large temple grounds. They have led to the inclusion of the Hōryū-ji in the World Cultural Heritage List. The wood construction method has proved to be resistant and is also well suited to the climate, but wooden buildings are liable to catch fire, and the earliest Hōryū-ji buildings fell victim to a blaze in 670. By 714, however, the temple complex had been reconstructed in the original style using cypress wood.

A roofed wall surrounds the entire grounds. In the south a two-storey gate building provides access to the interior, which consists of two separate temple areas. The most important buildings in the Hōryū-ji are located in the west of the complex. The Kondō, or Golden Hall, marks the centre of the temple. The two-storey structure rises over a rectangular ground plan, the top floor surmounted by a large roof with upturned corners. Believers walk clockwise around the most important sacred objects, namely devotional images and Buddha statues, which are on a raised platform in the Golden Hall. Passages and verandas sheltered by generous roofs encircle the central hall. The five-storey pagoda, which is also an important part of any Buddhist temple complex, is to the left of the Kondō. All four sides of the pagoda of the Hōryū-ji are decorated with clay sculptures that represent scenes from the life of the Buddha. The Great Lecture Hall, whose present incarnation dates to the 10th century, marks the end of the inner section of the temple. Additional buildings joined the Hōryū-ji ensemble over the course of the centuries, including two modern treasuries. The Eastern Temple area, on the other hand, was built as early as the 8th century and now occupies the space of the former prince's palace. This also consists of several architectural structures. The octagonal Yumedono, or Hall of Dreams, is at the centre. It contains a wooden sculpture from the 7th century that is part of the Japanese national heritage.

HŌRYŪ-JI, NARA, JAPAN, BEGUN IN THE 7TH CENTURY

'THIS DOME WAS BUILT BY THE SERVANT OF GOD ABD [AL-MALIK], COMMANDER OF THE FAITHFUL, IN THE YEAR SEVENTY-TWO, MAY GOD ACCEPT IT AND BE CONTENT WITH IT.'

Inscription above the cornice on the dome

DOME OF THE ROCK, JERUSALEM, COMPLETED IN AD 691/92

12

DOME OF THE ROCK, JERUSALEM

There can be few other places in the world that are of such great religious significance to as many people as the Temple Mount in Jerusalem, upon which the Dome of the Rock is built. According to legend, this place, and the holy rock in particular, was the site of important moments in the three great monotheistic world religions: Judaism, Christianity and Islam.

In the Old Testament, Abraham wanted to sacrifice his son Isaac here, and this is also where Solomon's Temple, which held the Ark of the Covenant, once stood. After the Babylonian Captivity, the Jews built another temple on this site, which was lavishly decorated by Herod and destroyed by the Romans in AD 70. Its remains now form the Western Wall. It was from this place that Mohammed set off on his nocturnal journey to heaven on a horse given to him by the Archangel Gabriel. During the Crusades, the Dome of the Rock was occupied by the Christians from 1099 to 1187, and a golden cross rose above its dome. This was replaced by a golden crescent moon by Saladin after the reconquest.

In Arabic, the Dome of the Rock is referred to simply as 'The Dome' (*qubba*). It is sometimes known as the 'Mosque of Omar', but this is actually incorrect as it was built not by Omar but by Caliph Abd al-Malik and also because the Dome of the Rock is not a mosque but a shrine for the holy rock at the centre of the structure.

The Dome of the Rock was completed in the year 72 according to the Islamic calendar, which corresponds to AD 691/92. That makes it one of the oldest and most important sacred Islamic architectural structures. It was built in the Umayyad style, whereby the architectural concept draws on early Christian Byzantine central-plan structures such as San Vitale in Ravenna and the rotunda of the Constantinian Church of the Holy Sepulchre in Jerusalem. At its centre lies the holy rock, surrounded by a central rotunda that is, in turn, surrounded by an octagonal arcade walkway. The columns originated in various Christian churches and are used here as spolia. The entire complex is contained within an even octagonal shape with a diameter of approximately 55 metres. The holy rock itself has a surface area measuring 18 by 13 metres, above which rises the eponymous dome (diameter: 20 metres). Its exterior is no longer made of black lead but has since 1993 been covered in gold-galvanised plates that sparkle in the sunshine.

The façade design using multicoloured marble in the vicinity of the base is a remnant of the original phase. The characteristic tile exterior was constructed from 1545 to 1566 under Sultan Suleiman the Magnificent and consists of an estimated 45,000 tiles. In 1960/61 the original tiles were removed and replaced with reproductions. The 240-metre-long frieze that encircles it features quotations from the Koran. In Islamic architecture, writing is an integral component that gives meaning to the structure, for pictorial representations, common in Christian art, are largely banned in Islamic art. Because of its exposed position, its golden dome and especially its significance, the Dome of the Rock is the most important landmark of Jerusalem.

TEMPLE I, TIKAL, GUATEMALA, COMPLETED IN 734

13

TEMPEL I, TIKAL

When the myth-enshrouded Mayans ruled Central America, Tikal was one of their powerful centres. In its golden age the city in the north of present-day Guatemala was home to 80,000 inhabitants. Ruins of the stone pyramids, temples and sculptures continue to tell the story of life in this important Mayan settlement.

Tikal, which lies amidst the rainforests of the province of Petén, is considered one of the most thoroughly studied Mayan cities. More than three thousand different architectural structures have been discovered there to date, including temples and palace complexes, as well as simple homes. A good deal is known about the city's numerous rulers, who had names as evocative as Smoking Frog, Dark Sun and Great Jaguar Paw.

The golden age of Tikal began in the 5th century, when temples and pyramids for the gods were built and hundreds of stone steles telling the story of the city and its rulers were erected. The Great Plaza, lined by altars and temples, was at the centre. These majestic buildings were commissioned by the 26th ruler of Tikal. They included the tall twin pyramids on the short sides of the square. Temple I on the east side rises towards the sky in nine stone steps. The ruler himself was ceremoniously buried in the richly decorated pyramid in the year 734, and among the burial objects placed in his tomb were more than 180 pieces of jewellery made from jade. This ruler, whose many names include Ah Cacau and Hasaw Kan K'awil, also commissioned the construction of the pyramid on the west side of the Great Plaza. Like its counterpart, it, too, consists of high terraces with projections and recesses in its walls. A steep set of steps leads up the wall overlooking the square. An enormous mask of a god embellishes the roof. On the north of the square lies the largest architectural ensemble of Tikal: grouped together on several levels on the North Acropolis are a number of temples and tombs, which used to be accessible via steps. A long row of steles and round altars memorialising the deceased rulers of Tikal stood in front of the great platform. The rulers lived in a palace complex on the south of the Great Plaza, where various residences extended around a total of six inner courtyards. The buildings, some of them multi-storey, housed audience halls and living quarters. Spectators could follow the ritual ball game held on specially constructed courts by the rulers in honour of the gods. Here, a rubber ball determined whether players lived or died. The highest temple pyramid of Tikal – and of Central America as a whole – is Temple IV, measuring almost 65 metres in height, in the west of the complex. It is the symbol of the reign of the 27th ruler of Tikal, Yik'in Chan K'awiil, and was constructed in the mid-8th century, by which time the golden age of Tikal was already over. The city subsequently fell into ruin, its population left, and the city was eventually deserted. The rainforest of Petén soon engulfed the temples and palaces. Systematic research into Tikal did not begin until the 1880s.

14

MEZQUITA, CÓRDOBA

One of the largest sacred architectural structures of the Islamic world is located at the heart of the historic centre of Córdoba. From the outside, the Mezquita compound looks rather like a fortress: high sandstone walls surmounted by parapets surround the rectangular building. However, visitors must step inside to see the great magnificence that developed under Islamic rule on the Iberian Peninsula.

When the Moors declared the southern Spanish city of Córdoba to be their capital in the year 711, the city entered a golden age: schools, libraries and colleges were built, mosques were constructed, hospitals and public baths were opened. In the 10th century, Córdoba had a population of more than half a million inhabitants. The history of the construction of the Great Mosque reflects the development of the city. The first emir of Córdoba, Abd al-Rahman I, laid the foundation stone for the Mezquita. The 11-aisled mosque with its open courtyard was built over the course of just one year, starting in 785. As the Islamic community grew rapidly, the building was soon too small. Successive rulers expanded the complex: the prayer hall grew substantially, the mosque's courtyard was expanded and a new minaret was erected. After four expansions, the gigantic surface area covered by the Mezquita finally measured 22,000 square metres.

The main entrance, the Puerta del Perdón, lies on the north side of the complex. It leads into the arcade-lined courtyard, the Patio de los Naranjos. The orange trees here were not planted until the 19th century. In Moorish times the courtyard was planted with palms, and at its centre stood wells for the ritual cleansing of the faithful before prayer. The interior is a veritable forest of columns that form endless rows of arcades decorated with artistic ornamentation and calligraphy. The horseshoe-shaped double arches consist of two colours, with blocks of red brick and light sandstone alternating. Countless columns, of which there were more than a thousand originally, fell prey to later alterations to the building. In 1236 the city was conquered by Catholic kings. They did not destroy the Great Mosque but instead consecrated it as a Christian cathedral and added numerous chapels to it. In the 16th century an enormous cathedral was eventually constructed in the former prayer hall, yet the most important architectural element of the prayer hall, the mihrab, has been preserved. The octagonal prayer niche is richly ornamented and surmounted by a shell-shaped dome. The artistic architectural ornamentation was commissioned by the second caliph of Córdoba, Al-Hakam II. He asked the Byzantine emperor to recommend a mosaic artist who would instruct the local craftsmen in this technique. According to an inscription, the lavishly decorated mihrab was completed in 965. A horseshoe-shaped arch forms the entrance to the niche. Above it is a decorative area on which colourful mosaics form ornaments and writing on a gold ground. Since pictorial representations of God are forbidden in Islam, both writing and geometric and floral elements became an essential form of artistic expression. The walls and ceiling of the Great Mosque, too, are decorated with multicoloured construction materials, delicate ornaments made of stone and stucco, as well as numerous inscriptions.

'THE TEXTURE OF A COLUMN IN THE MEZQUITA IS A NUANCE OF REALITY, AND HE WHO HAS ONCE SET EYES ON IT WILL NEVER FORGET IT. IT TAKES POSSESSION OF HIS ENTIRE MEMORY.'

Jorge Luis Borges

MEZQUITA, CÓRDOBA, BEGUN IN 785

left The double horseshoe arches of the Mezquita dominated the visual impression of the prayer hall of the former mosque. They line the imposing space in long rows. Horseshoe-shaped arches were commonly used in Islamic architecture in Spain.

above The ruler's place of prayer was under the ribbed dome of the maqsura. Following the reconquest of Córdoba by the Christians the Mezquita was consecrated as a church, though only a small number of structural changes were carried out. It was not until the 16th century that the Bishop of Córdoba ordered a nave to be built into the interior of the Mezquita.

MEZQUITA, CÓRDOBA, BEGUN IN 785

BOROBUDUR, JAVA, INDONESIA, CIRCA 750–850

15

BOROBUDUR, JAVA

In 1814 archaeologists discovered an unusually high number of chiselled blocks of stone in the rice paddies of the Indonesian island of Java. The find would prove spectacular. Hidden beneath a layer of volcanic ash and the lush plant world of the tropical surroundings, one of the biggest Buddhist temples in the world lay dormant: the hill of the gods named Borobudur.

The temple of Borobudur was constructed between 750 and 850, during the reign of the Sailendra kings. The Buddhist rulers used imposing temple constructions to shore up their power over central Java. The largest of these, Borobudur, is reached via a pilgrim path lined with temples. The pyramid-like shape of Borobudur itself rises above a natural hill. It grows out of a square footprint, each side measuring 110 metres. Its seven steps are made of approximately two million stone blocks. The structure is solid, containing no hollow spaces. Stairs and step-like gates connect the various levels with one another, all of which are made of exposed stone. The lower area consists of four rectangular galleries, above which there are three round terraces. The three concentric circles at the top feature 72 stupas, or stone memorials, each containing a sculpture of a seated Buddha. The solid central stupa, whose diameter measures about 10 metres, rises above the highest level of the temple.

Buddhist ritual dictates that believers walk along the structure's terraces in a clockwise direction. They thus walk past the reliefs carved into the stone that decorate the inner walls of the gallery-like ambulatories measuring more than five kilometres in length. The complex iconographic programme encompasses some 1,300 scenic representations and countless other decorative reliefs. The life of the historical Buddha is told on the lowest level of the temple, combined with many depictions of courtly and agricultural life in Java in the 8th and 9th centuries. The more than five hundred earlier existences of the Buddha are represented further up. The three highest terraces eschew all pictorial narrative: this is where the 72 smaller stupas with their seated Buddha figures are located. They show the pilgrims the way towards eternal bliss, which is known as Nirvana. The great main stupa at the centre of the temple symbolises enlightenment. In its square ground plan and layout, the temple of Borobudur corresponds to a Buddhist mandala on an enormous scale. This much researchers can agree upon. The history of the creation and function of the temple, however, are still very opaque. Whether it was a monastery, a burial site, or whether the temple served first and foremost as a demonstration of power remains a subject of debate to this day.

left Relics and representations of the Buddha are kept in the stupas. A total of 72 of these stone memorials surround the temple's three terraces in concentric circles in Borobudur, the largest of all Buddhist sacred structures.

above A sophisticated iconographic programme transforms the divine elevation of Borobudur into a picture book, with more than 1,300 scenes not only telling stories from the life of the Buddha, but also depicting everyday life from Java in the 8th and 9th centuries.

BOROBUDUR, JAVA, INDONESIA, CIRCA 750–850

SAN MINIATO AL MONTE, FLORENCE, 11TH/12TH CENTURY

16

SAN MINIATO AL MONTE, FLORENCE

The small church of San Miniato al Monte is dedicated to St Minias, an Armenian prince who was tortured and then beheaded for his faith by Emperor Decius in circa AD 250. According to legend, Florence's first martyr then tucked his head under his arm and walked up Mons Fiorentius, where he was to be buried.

The present-day church was built in 1013, after the destruction of its predecessor. The façade is one of the most beautiful and balanced examples of Italian Romanesque architecture, for which the Swiss art historian Jacob Burckhardt (1818–1897) coined the term 'proto-Renaissance'. This style consists of ancient Roman architectural motifs combined with sophisticated elegance, primarily in Tuscany as well as in Provence. It is rare among the more fortress-like buildings of the Romanesque style in the rest of Europe. Alongside the Florence Baptistery, San Miniato is an outstanding example.

The effect of the white marble and green serpentine on the façade is at once opulent and balanced. The upper storey, whose centre is occupied by a mosaic dating to 1260 that represents Christ as the judge of the world, rises above five blind arcades on Corinthian half-columns. The upper storey is enlivened with fluted pilasters and surmounted by a gable upon whose tip stands an eagle digging its claws into a bale of wool. This is the emblem of the cloth merchants' guild, which was responsible for the upkeep of the church from 1288.

The entire façade is richly embellished with geometric patterns that reach up as far as the blind dwarf gallery along the gable and the finely chased patterns above. This graphic geometric decoration extends into the interior, which was built according to the three-aisle design with the timber truss roof typical of early Christian basilicas.

The heavier columns interrupt the uniform series of Corinthian pillars and also feature diaphragm arches decorated with geometric designs. The marble inlay work also continues along the clerestory. The space, whose sidewalls are at present bare as a result of restoration work, gives the impression of being extraordinarily harmonious and light.

The elevated choir is located in front of the semicircular apse. Most of the mortal remains of the martyr are thought to be buried in the crypt below (parts of the relics were taken to Metz in the 10th century). Important Florentine artists were repeatedly commissioned to work on the church. These included Michelozzo, who in 1488 took the unusual decision to build the Capella dello Crocefisso in the centre of the nave, and Luca della Robbia, who created the terracotta decoration. Frescos by Taddeo Gaddi can be seen in the crypt.

The building that abuts the church on the right, at the other end of a connecting structure, is the Florentine bishop's palace, which was constructed between 1294 and 1320.

San Miniato, this gem of the Florentine proto-Renaissance, looks down on the city from its high vantage point. Its wealth of graphic decoration and simultaneous austerity in particular had a profound influence on later Florentine architects such as Filippo Brunelleschi, Michelangelo and, most significantly, Leon Battista Alberti.

The **GUILD SYSTEM** in Florence developed in the late 12th century and had a considerable influence on the city's society and economy. There were seven major guilds (Arti Maggiori), which represented the interests of physicians, the legal professions and merchants, including the cloth merchants' guild (Arte di Calimala). Craftsmen, innkeepers and retailers belonged to the 14 minor guilds (Arti Minori). Aside from ensuring compliance with the specific regulations governing the various professions, the guilds also represented the interests of their members in the municipal government and were responsible for communal tasks such as the construction and maintenance of a variety of buildings, from the Baptistery to the Basilica di Santa Maria del Fiore.

17

CATHEDRAL OF ST MARY AND ST STEPHEN, SPEYER

German emperors starting with Charlemagne revived the idea of the Roman Empire. The Carolingians and Ottonians were succeeded by the Salian dynasty when Konrad II (990–1039) ascended to the throne of the Holy Roman Empire. He, too, believed that his legitimacy was derived from the tradition of the Roman Empire, and was crowned emperor in Rome in 1027.

Konrad ordered the cathedral of St Mary and St Stephen in Speyer to be built so as to demonstrate this imperial claim in a suitably impressive manner. The cathedral of Speyer, which measured 134 metres in length and thus became the largest ecclesiastical building of the Holy Roman Empire, was not to be a mere episcopal church, however. It was also to be the burial place of the Salian dynasty – in other words, an imperial cathedral.

Work began in 1025 with a three-aisled, flat-roofed basilica with a separated crossing and an imposing westwork. Neither Konrad nor his son, Heinrich III (1017–1056), lived to see the completion of the cathedral, which was consecrated more than three decades later in the year 1061. The imperial Roman claim was already expressed in this first structure, referred to as 'Speyer 1' by architectural historians. It is remarkable not only for its size, but also, and most importantly, for its modern, seminal concept. Whereas the nave of earlier Romanesque churches was divided into the ground-floor arcades and a two-dimensional clerestory wall, in Speyer 1, both storeys were combined by monumental transverse arches. This created an entirely novel vertical accent, which became the architectural leitmotif of Speyer. It creates the impression of enormous arcades reminiscent of Roman aqueducts in their 12-fold sequence. The blind arcades are not merely superimposed, however, but grow out of the square piers and extend the piers upwards. The arcade and clerestory wall thus recedes and becomes a 'filler' of the gaps in a lattice. This is an early form of skeleton construction, which would soon shape the future.

Konrad's grandson, Heinrich IV (1050–1106), made changes to the cathedral from 1082 to 1106 ('Speyer II'). A dome was constructed above the crossing, the choir received a semicircular apse, and a dwarf gallery was added around the exterior, but the most important change concerned the nave. Whereas only aisles had been vaulted in the past, the nave, too, was now vaulted. This was achieved by adding a pilaster with an engaged half-column to every second nave pier. This resulted in a dynamic alternation of supports and rectangular bays that were surmounted by groin vaults. This, too, had not been seen since antiquity and was of seminal importance.

The claim to the inheritance of the Roman Empire was no longer exerted by copying Roman architecture but by building an independent structure that aimed to surpass those of Rome. The effort and technical innovations that were repeatedly brought to bear on the cathedral of Speyer over the centuries are certainly worthy of an imperial cathedral.

In its current incarnation, Speyer Cathedral is in large parts the result of century-long construction and reconstruction. Fortunately, those in charge always took care not to disfigure the original structure. When renovations were carried out by Balthasar Neumann's son in the 18th century, the urge to add Baroque elements was resisted in favour of a new approach: restorative cultural-heritage conservation.

THE CATHEDRAL OF ST MARY AND ST STEPHEN, SPEYER, CONSECRATED IN 1061

'GREY TOWERS OF DURHAM
YET WELL I LOVE THY MIXED AND MASSIVE PILES
HALF CHURCH OF GOD, HALF CASTLE 'GAINST THE SCOT'

Sir Walter Scott

DURHAM CATHEDRAL, BEGUN IN 1093

18

DURHAM CATHEDRAL

Fans of Harry Potter will immediately recognise Durham Cathedral. In the film versions of the fantasy novels, it houses the Hogwarts School of Witchcraft and Wizardry. It is against this spectacular backdrop that the talented apprentice wizard Harry learns the countless tricks of his trade.

Harry lets owls fly over the snow-covered inner courtyard of the cloisters, and the young wizards and witches explore the art of transformation in the cathedral's chapter-house. The stage provided by the mediaeval church in the northern English city of Durham has a much longer history, however: Benedictine monks founded the abbey on a cliff above the River Wear in the 10th century. The church would eventually house the mortal remains of the holy Bishop Cuthbert, and a great number of pilgrims came to visit what were at the time the most important relics on the island.

After the Normans had conquered England in 1066, they began to cover the entire country with buildings whose aim was to reflect their power. In 1093 work also began on the monumental cathedral of Durham, which was built on the site of its predecessor. Construction on this enormous building site continued far into the 13th century. The view of the exterior of the building, which measures more than 140 metres in length, is governed by solid walls. The imposing west façade is dominated by two towers. A tall crossing tower rises above the place where a wide crossbar intersects with the nave and two aisles. From the outside the church certainly looks like a fortress, and this is no coincidence: after all, the rebellious Scots were not far away.

The tomb of St Cuthbert lies in the east of the building, the choir. The architects developed a new ceiling structure for this section, which contrasts markedly with the heavy-set Romanesque forms that characterise the rest of the building. High vaulting now took the place of the flat roofs that had until then been in common usage. Ribs divide the vaulted ceiling into four bays, and narrow ribs, which separate the severies, are set underneath these corners. This form of vaulting, which was first showcased in Durham, is known as cross-ribbed vaulting. The advances made by the cathedral architects in the art of vaulting are not confined to the choir: the church in Durham is in fact the first large High Romanesque architectural structure to be entirely covered with vaulted ceilings. The forms on the interior of the impressive building draw heavily on Norman art, which reached England together with the cathedral architecture of the Norman conquerors. The wall of the nave is divided into three zones, with the arch of the lower section supported by mighty pillars that measure up to six metres in circumference. They are decorated with a variety of patterns, including the diamonds and zigzag shapes that are typical of the Norman style. UNESCO regards Durham Cathedral as the perfect memorial to Norman architecture in England and included the church on its list of World Cultural Heritage sites for this reason in 1986.

The **ROMANESQUE** period owes its name to its references to ancient Rome, such as round arches, the technique for which was already known in Roman architecture. The most important construction projects of the Romanesque period were churches and monasteries. These were built based on the architectural type of the basilica, with a central nave, two aisles and a semicircular apse. The portals and façades of the churches were embellished with a wealth of architectural details: large interior and exterior walls featuring only a small number of small windows offered ample space for such ornamentation. The Romanesque period saw an important innovation in ceiling construction. Over time, the ceilings above the naves became vaulted. The term 'Romanesque' came into common usage in the 19th century to describe the period of art history covering the 11th to the mid-13th century.

Durham Cathedral is an early example of the Romanesque art of vaulting. The vaulted ceilings transfer their weight to the walls' pillars and columns. The space between them has essentially been dissolved and is also richly orna-mented.

DURHAM CATHEDRAL, BEGUN IN 1093

SAINT-ÉTIENNE, CAEN, CONSECRATED IN 1081

19

SAINT-ÉTIENNE, CAEN

In 1049 William (1027–1087), Duke of Normandy and later conqueror and king of England, was planning his wedding to Matilda of Flanders (circa 1030/31–1083). Pope Leo IX forbade them from marrying, however, on the grounds that they were too closely related. They married in 1051 all the same, and were excommunicated. It was not until 1059 that the marriage was approved by Pope Nicholas II. In penance for their transgression, William and Matilda agreed to found the monastery of Saint-Étienne for monks and the monastery of Sainte-Trinité for nuns.

As was generally the case with royal endowments, expectations were very high, and it is likely that they were further elevated by internal competition between the two architectural projects. These expectations were not only met, but exceeded, in particular where Saint-Étienne was concerned. The church, which was consecrated in 1081, became the main representative building and constitutes the pinnacle of Romanesque architecture in Normandy. A three-tier wall structure with arcades, galleries and a double-walled clerestory rises above the floor plan of a three-aisled basilica with a protruding transept. This structure with the galleries above the aisles lends this sophisticated building a distinctive spatial character in comparison with simpler Romanesque churches. As a result, the nave has a less domineering presence and the semicircular engaged arcade pillars are emphasised. This led to an increasing 'dissolution of the wall' in favour of an emphasis on the skeleton-construction method, which had begun with the cathedral of Speyer (see page 50) and its system of support and filler. This process of the 'dissolution of the wall', which would culminate in the High Gothic style, began its conquest with Speyer in the east and Saint-Étienne in the west. In circa 1120 the original flat roof was replaced by the first ribbed vaulting in France. The exterior, too, with its imposing two-tower façade in the west, became a prototype of the classic two-tower façade, which came to replace the early Romanesque westwork. The front of the nave and the towers have a common vanishing point, and the nave and aisles correspond to the three portals on the exterior. This is reflected in the storeyed horizontal structure, and the flying buttresses, whose purpose is to support the weight of the towers, vertically divide the façade. The two towers, which also feature dominant vertical tiers, rise above the façade block. The number of windows set into the walls increases towards the top. The pointed spires date to the 13th century, which is also when the original stepped choir was replaced by a Gothic ambulatory.

This combination of towers and a longitudinal plan at Saint-Étienne was found to be the appropriate façade form for a basilica. It would soon become widespread and reached its apogee in the elaborate west façades of Gothic cathedrals. As had been the case with the cathedral of Speyer, the requirements of a ruler's church were undoubtedly also exceeded with Saint-Étienne in Caen. William the Conqueror, as he came to be known after 1066, was be buried there in 1087.

WILLIAM THE CONQUEROR was born in circa 1027 in Falaise (Calvados), the illegitimate son of Robert I. He became Duke of Normandy in 1035. He landed with this army in Sussex in 1066, and was victorious over the Anglo-Saxon King Harold II, or Harold Godwinson, at the Battle of Hastings on 14 October. He was crowned King of England on Christmas Day that same year. He later commissioned the famous, 70-metre-long *Bayeux Tapestry*, which paints an impressive picture of the Norman conquest of England.

'BRITAIN WILL FALL
IF THE RAVENS LEAVE THE TOWER'

Old saying

THE WHITE TOWER, LONDON, BEGUN IN 1078

20

WHITE TOWER, LONDON

Following the conquest of England by William, Duke of Normandy (1027–1087), the future king of England set about subjugating the whole country, which he achieved by 1071. He could not feel entirely secure, however, so he built a fortress – the Tower of London – 'against the fickleness of the great and wild masses' on a hill on the south-east edge of the London of his time.

The advantages of this site were obvious. It provided an unobstructed view of the Thames and made it possible to react quickly to threats posed by ships sailing upriver. William summoned a specialist from his native region for this task: Gundulf, a Norman monk and later bishop of Rochester, who had gained some experience in the construction of churches and castles in Normandy. He built a fortress that corresponded to the keeps and fortified towers of the Normans.

Two main storeys rise above the ground floor with the undercroft and the well, which was essential for survival. The footprint is virtually square, measuring 36 by 32.5 metres. The entrance is located on the first floor and was accessible via wooden steps. The buttresses in the walls reinforce the structure and subdivide the façade. The White Tower, which is 27.5 metres high, is crowned by the corner towers and the battlements that connect them. The Tower has stood as a symbol of power and might ever since its construction.

As is also the case with the Norman castles on the mainland, the south-east corner of the Tower features a chapel that consists of two storeys, like the models upon which it is based. The Tower was completed after a construction period of 20 years, and although it was frequently expanded and adapted to suit changing needs, the defensive capabilities of the core structure always remained central features. It was given the name 'White Tower' after it had been painted in the 13th century. This was when Henry III built the first wall around it. The wall was completed and expanded to its present dimensions through the addition of a second wall by his son Edward I. The second wall served an important function: to entrap any attackers who managed to clamber over it. This, too, helped to make the Tower impregnable.

The 'Norman style' remained dominant in English architecture until William's death. For the conquerors, architecture served more than just a pragmatic purpose; it was also a symbol of their military and cultural superiority.

The **WHITE TOWER** was the first important secular architectural structure to be built in England after the Romans' departure from the island. For centuries it was used not only as the royal palace, but also as an arsenal, prison, mint and, since the time of Henry III, as an animal enclosure that is considered to have been the first public zoo. The last of the beasts in the royal menagerie were transferred to London Zoo in 1835. The Tower has also housed the treasury and the Crown Jewels since 1841. The traditional gate-locking Ceremony of the Keys has taken place at the Tower every evening for the past 700 years. The warders are also known as 'Beefeaters', possibly a corruption of the French term *bouffetier*, which means cupbearer, and because their services were once paid for in beef.

'AT PISA WE CLIMBED UP TO THE TOP OF
THE STRANGEST STRUCTURE THE WORLD HAS ANY KNOWLEDGE OF–
THE LEANING TOWER.'

Mark Twain

SANTA MARIA ASSUNTA, CONSECRATED IN 1118, AND CAMPANILE, BEGUN IN 1173, PISA

21

SANTA MARIA ASSUNTA AND CAMPANILE, PISA

Never has a building been more famous for its completely unsuitable substrate than the Leaning Tower of Pisa. Had it been built on normal substrate, and not on Pisa's alluvial plains, it would be beautiful, but it would not lean.

The Campanile is only one part of the impressive sacred complex, whose buildings, in accordance with mediaeval beliefs, represent the symbolic path from inclusion in the community of the faithful to paradise. It includes the baptistery (1152–1380), the cathedral, the Campanile and the graveyard (1278–83). No wonder that the Italian poet Gabriele D'Annunzio referred to the area as the Piazza dei Miracoli, or Square of Miracles.

The first phase of the cathedral's construction lasted from 1063 to its consecration in 1118. This resulted in the creation of a three-aisled, flat-roofed basilica. It was expanded between 1150 and 1200 to its present size. This led to the elaborate, five-aisled basilica with a three-aisled transept and a choir. Not only the monolithic granite columns that line the nave, but also the double galleries, which extend across two storeys, are unusual.

The oval crossing dome is even more extraordinary for this period.

Four rows of columns superimposed like a lattice over the actual wall rise above seven blind arcades with three inset bronze doors on the façade. In addition to the dazzlingly white marble, it is the presence of these vaulted galleries that imbues the architectural structures on the Piazza dei Miracoli with a homogenous air despite the long construction time.

The construction of the Campanile began in 1173 and lasted, with several interruptions, for some 200 years. The tower was furnished with the same blind vaulted arcades as the cathedral. When the fourth storey had almost been completed in 1178, it already leaned 90 centimetres to one side. This was due to the fact that the ground became compacted under the weight, causing it to sag. After a 100-year wait, construction continued with a small corrective measure. When the seventh storey had been completed in 1278, the tower leaned yet further, and the builders waited again for the ground to settle. The bell chamber was finally completed between 1360 and 1370.

The various attempts to straighten the tower are visible both on the outside and on the steps inside. Over the course of time, the tower, which weighs 14,500 tonnes, has sunk approximately three metres into the ground. In 1838 the tower plinths and the foundation-wall steps were exposed (to make the tower look the way it was originally supposed to look), causing it to lean even further. By 1990, it was leaning three metres off the perpendicular, and in 2001 it was closed so that stabilisation measures could be carried out. By removing soil, the Campanile was lowered further in order to straighten it. This procedure can theoretically be repeated, but as the ground on which it stands will always remain unstable and the structure is extremely susceptible, it is perhaps only a matter of time before it requires an external support – or does indeed topple over.

GIOVANNI PISANO (circa 1250– after 1314) came from a famous family of sculptors and was one of the greatest sculptors of his time. His realistic and dramatic methods opened up new possibilities for sculptural design. He created, amongst other things, the cathedral pulpit in Pisa (1302–11).

22

SAN MARCO, VENICE

As in many cities, the relics of Venice's patron saint arrived here by dubious means. According to legend, Mark the Evangelist had – on one of his many missionary journeys several centuries earlier – come to the Venetian Lagoon, where an angel told him his remains would one day be buried here.

In 828 the time had come: shortly after the founding of Venice, Venetian merchants stole the relics of the saint in Alexandria and brought them to Venice on a hair-raising journey (hidden beneath pieces of pork to prevent Muslims from looking too closely). In Venice, a church dedicated to him was immediately built, and he replaced St Theodore as the city's patron saint. From that point onwards the Venetian lion, the symbol of the evangelist and henceforth also that of Venice, reigned over the eastern Mediterranean. The church burned down in 976, and construction on the present-day cathedral began in 1063. The relics of the evangelist had in the meantime been lost and, miraculously, refound, so that the new church building could be consecrated in the year 1094. St Mark's Cathedral is a cross-in-square church with the floor plan of a Greek cross. Its clearly structured main body was initially free-standing, however. In its present form San Marco is a reflection of its long construction history, which was shaped by a variety of influences, as well as extensions and alterations. Every element of this church points to its architectural affinity with the East, which was virtually inevitable owing to the city's economic ties. It drew inspiration from Justinian's Church of the Holy Apostles in Constantinople, which was destroyed by the Ottomans in the 15th century. San Marco is the only one of the Byzantine great churches to have survived. The two-storey west façade with its five portals decorated with columns and the narrow porch (narthex) in the north were added in the 13th century and underscored the status of the church as a state church and a Venetian national treasure. The majority of the many columns that embellish the portals are spolia from various conquests. The hemispherical domes that draw on Byzantine models and with which the church dominates the view of the Piazza San Marco were built at the same time as the porch. The appearance of the cathedral in the mid-13th century is accurately reproduced in the mosaics of the first narthex portal: the Porta di Sant'Alipio. Visitors enter the church's interior, which is entirely covered in marble and mosaics, through the porch, which is also decorated with mosaics. Measuring more than 8,000 square metres, it is one of the largest contiguous mosaic-covered surfaces in the world. The complex architecture with its pillars, columns, niches and domes, the opulent decoration with marble and mosaics and the dim light give visitors the impression that they truly have stumbled into an oversize treasure chest.

The famous **QUADRIGA** above the main portal was plundered after the victory over Byzantium in 1204. It is believed to have originally embellished Nero's triumphal arch in Rome. After Napoleon's occupation of Venice in 1797, the four bronze horses were shipped off to Paris, but the Congress of Vienna ordered their return in 1815. It is the only extant classical quadriga and is now housed in the Museo San Marco – a replica of the original having taken its place on the façade.

'THE FIRST IMPRESSION IS THAT OF ... A CAVE OF MIRACLES,
OF THE TREASURE CHEST OF AN AGEING PRINCE OF PIRATES
WHO HAS COME TO BE IMBUED WITH GENTLE MAGICAL POWERS.
IT DRIPS WITH GOLD AND THE LIGHT IS WARM AND SLIGHTLY BROWN.'

Herbert Rosendorfer

SAN MARCO, VENICE, CONSECRATED IN 1094

23

CATHEDRAL OF SAINT-DENIS

Time and again there are buildings of great significance that have a profound influence on the history of architecture. The cathedral of the former Benedictine abbey of Saint-Denis on the outskirts of Paris is one of them.

In the Middle Ages, Saint-Denis was the religious and occasionally also the political centre of the French monarchy. This is where the relics of the apostle and patron saint of France, St Dionysius, are kept. It was the burial site of French rulers and, as a royal abbey, was under the direct control of the Crown. The monastery's abbot, Suger (1081–1151), was one of the most influential men of his time – a friend and advisor to Louis VI and, for a period of time, even regent of the realm. The Carolingian architectural structure dating to the 8th century was subjected to revolutionary alterations in accordance with his wishes. Under Abbot Suger, Saint-Denis became the first building of the Gothic period.

Gothic architecture is known to be characterised by three main elements: cross-ribbed vaulting, pointed arches and the system of buttresses and flying buttresses. None of these characteristic elements was an invention of the Gothic period, however, for each of them already existed in earlier buildings. What makes Saint-Denis novel and revolutionary is the combination of these elements in order to realise an entirely new architectural concept. To this end, Suger drew on the writings on the metaphysics of light by the mystic Dionysius the Areopagite (5th century), in whose opinion light was the unmediated apparition of the divine.

First of all, the façade was altered between 1137 and 1140. It is modelled on the double-tower concept of Norman churches such as Saint-Étienne in Caen (see page 56), but reinterprets them so that the towers and the façade block no longer appear to be separate, but instead constitute a unit. For the very first time, the central rosette becomes a façade motif, as do the column figures by the entrance portal. This type of façade became a model for later Gothic churches and cathedrals.

In 1140 work on the towers was interrupted and was begun instead on the liturgical and aesthetic heart of the cathedral: the choir. Suger planned a double ambulatory with radiating chapels subdivided only by buttresses. Saint-Denis features the first use in central Europe of pointed arches, so typical of the Gothic period. Its choir was the first to be furnished with cross-ribbed vaulting. This extraordinary choir was completed remarkably quickly, between July 1140 and October 1143. Only the double ambulatory and radiating chapels remain, however, as the choir itself was demolished to make way for High Gothic alterations to the church (1231–81). The fact that all of the dioceses represented at the consecration ceremony in 1144 very soon began to build a Gothic cathedral filled with the 'eternal light of the Godhead' is testament to the success and influence of the new architectural concept. Abbot Suger and his (unfortunately unknown) architect succeeded here in creating that which makes Saint-Denis so important in the history of architecture. He combined the individual parts of the architectural structure to form a new overall concept in which light occupies a central role both from a theological perspective and as a design principle. Suger wanted 'wonderful and uninterrupted' light throughout the church's interior, and the Gothic skeleton system perfectly suited this purpose. The resulting 'dissolution of the wall' freed up space that Suger filled with glass surfaces. The diaphanously lit space enabled him to transform the 'theology of light' into an 'architecture of light'.

'IF ONE SEARCHES FOR AN IDEAL STARTING POINT FROM WHICH
THE GOTHIC UNFOLDED IN ITS ESSENTIALITY, ONE MUST LOOK TO THE
CHOIR AREA AS A CULTIC CENTRE.

Hans Jantzen

THE CATHEDRAL OF SAINT-DENIS, CONSECRATED IN 1144

'IN THIS YEAR FOR THE FIRST TIME AT CHARTRES ONE COULD SEE
THE FAITHFUL HARNESS CARTS TO THEMSELVES, LADEN WITH
STONES, WOOD, CORN AND WHATEVER ELSE WOULD BE NEEDED TO WORK ON THE CATHEDRAL.
THE TOWERS GREW UPWARDS AS IF BY MAGIC.'

Robert of Torigni, Abbot of Mont Saint-Michel

THE CATHEDRAL OF NOTRE-DAME DE CHARTRES, CONSECRATED IN 1260

24

CATHEDRAL OF NOTRE-DAME DE CHARTRES

Things might have turned out differently if the buildings that once stood on the space now occupied by the cathedral of Chartres had been dedicated to St Florian, the patron saint of firefighters. His patrocinium might have protected the five churches that had burned to the ground there since the 4th century.

In the year 1134 the entire city of Chartres was ravaged by fire, though only the north tower and the porch of the Romanesque cathedral were destroyed. The tower was immediately rebuilt, and the three-winged Royal Portal was placed between the two towers. In 1194 another blaze almost fully destroyed the Romanesque church's nave, as a result of which construction began on the new, Gothic cathedral. From the start, the west façade, the extant Romanesque crypt and the foundation determined the dimensions of the new building. This key work of classic Gothic architecture was constructed here by 1260.

In the ground plan, the architect successfully combined a three-aisled basilica with a five-aisled elongated choir and a double ambulatory and radiating chapels. Many cathedrals were not attached to a monastery but belonged to the city and were built not only for the greater glory of God, but also as an expression of civic pride. The cathedral of Chartres is dedicated to St Mary and houses the gown that the Mother of God is said to have worn during the Annunciation, an important Christian relic. Relics and the associated status as a place of pilgrimage were always an important source of income for cities and cathedrals in the Middle Ages. A sufficiently large ambulatory was therefore important because it made it possible to manage the crowds of pilgrims.

In the interior, the architect dispensed with the use of galleries in favour of a new three-partite wall structure consisting of the arcade, triforium (a passage above the arcade and below the clerestory that is open to the nave) and a clerestory that would go on to serve as a model for other churches. The result was a remarkable verticality heightened even further by the subsumption and simplification of the construction units. This was complemented by the newly conceived system of open buttresses, which made it possible to open up the walls and thus realise Abbot Suger's ideas about an 'architecture of light' even more effectively (see page 64).

Chartres probably comes closest to providing an accurate impression of what a Gothic cathedral originally looked like in terms of architecture and, above all else, the glass windows. This is because, unlike other churches in previous centuries, it did not burn down. Its wealth of sculptural decorations and glass windows even survived the French Revolution. Of the original windows, 186 – approximately 3,000 square metres of glass – have withstood the passage of time. During the Second World War, they were dismantled and put into safe storage.

The original plan for the cathedral provided for a total of nine towers. As in the case of numerous other cathedrals, this was not realised, however. Attention was clearly focused on high naves and ever higher flying buttresses, with which the cathedrals dominated the cities even without additional towers. They were supplemented with elaborately designed portals, whose complex iconographic programmes drew the visitor's attention to the sculptures. The cathedral of Chartres is a fine example of the Gothic style, which spread across all of Europe in the 13th century.

'THIS CLUSTER OF BUILDINGS GLEAMS MAGNIFICENTLY
IN THE FIRE OF THE PARCHING SUN, WHICH SHINES FROM THE ZENITH
WHILE BROKEN STONES, STATUES AND LIONS' BODIES
LIE HIDDEN IN THE GRASS AROUND US.'

Louis Delaporte

ANGKOR WAT, CAMBODIA, 1ST HALF OF THE 12TH CENTURY

25

ANGKOR WAT, CAMBODIA

The most famous sacred architectural structure of Cambodia was for a long time hidden in the depths of the jungle. It was not until the 19th century that the French explorer Henri Mouhot made the temple complex of Angkor Wat famous in Europe. In doing so, he awakened a wave of admiration for the culture of the Khmer, who built the gigantic temple at the centre of their empire.

At its apogee, the Khmer empire ruled present-day Cambodia along with parts of Vietnam and of Thailand. The Khmer established rice cultivation as an economic foundation and perfected it using a sophisticated irrigation system of rivers, canals and reservoirs. As their wealth grew through trade, the Khmer expanded their empire – and built lots of temples. Angkor Wat is the largest of these. The temple complex took shape in the first half of the 12th century. South of the old capital of Angkor Thom, the Khmer mapped out the enormous dimensions of the construction project with which King Suryavarman II would underscore his power. The names of all of the architects who designed the rectangular area measuring a total of almost 200 square kilometres are unknown, as are the names of all of the labourers, thousands of whom worked together to construct the gigantic complex of sandstone.

Eleven kilometres of water channels and reservoirs surround the temple, providing evidence of the Khmers' sophisticated engineering skills. The principal axis of the complex runs from west to east, with the main portal lying in the west. The central temple tower, surrounded by another four towers, is built on a platform measuring an impressive 365 by 250 metres, and rises in three steps to a height of 65 metres. The sculptural decorations of the complex, too, are impressive. The richly ornamented portal constitutes the entrance to a world of stone reliefs, balustrades and columns, decorated portals, corner towers, pedestals and roofs. The several-kilometre-long surrounding walls, like the main façade, are embellished with stone reliefs. As processions passed along them, the participants read the lively scenes representing Hindu and Buddhist subjects. The mythological representation of heaven and hell is dominated by the Hindu deity Vishnu, to whom the temple was dedicated. Historical wars and battles complete the extensive iconographic programme.

The temple city was also an expression of royal power. And this power was extensive as the king had to guarantee universal order. This interpretation also explains the dimensions of the temple complex. Numerous details relating to the function of the structure and its symbolic context, however, continue to give rise to speculation today. One thing is certain, though: the gigantic temple complex is clearly a magnificent testament to Khmer architecture.

left Five monumental towers rise above the enormous temple complex of Angkor Wat. Dating to the 12th century, it represents the pinnacle of Khmer architectural achievement.

above The stone reliefs cover hundreds of metres. They show scenes from Hindu mythology, processions and a bounty of ornamental decorations.

26

CASTEL DEL MONTE, ANDRIA

We are not sure whether the man who commissioned the fort on the mountain, Friedrich II – the last Hohenstaufen emperor – ever visited it, despite the fact that he clearly cared deeply about the castle in southern Italy. The Stauferkaiser was even said to have been involved in its planning.

Friedrich also commissioned other buildings. During his reign, a whole network of castles was built across southern Italy. But it is his Castel del Monte that presents academics with the biggest riddles. It lies on a hilltop in the bleak Apulian countryside, a few kilometres from the coast of the Adriatic. The castle was built in around 1240. Its ground plan is an octagon. Eight corner towers, also with an octagonal ground plan, surround the central building. The entrance to the castle complex lies on the east side, where visitors pass through into the octagonal inner courtyard. Arranged around it, on two floors, are eight vaulted rooms of equal size. The corridor system is carefully planned. Not all the rooms are directly linked with each other.

The smooth sandstone blocks of the masonry underline the massive impression of the building. The few decorative elements contrast with the yellowish glow of the stone. With its gable and a moulded frame, the entrance portal, for example, recalls antique forms – the emperor left his guests in no doubt as to his claims to sovereignty. Cut into the areas of wall between the towers are a few small windows. On the upper floor, these are decorated with pointed arches resting on slender pillars. Like the portal, Friedrich had them hewn from a particular stone, the reddish marble known as 'Breccia corallina': in this particular form of stone, white stone of various shapes and sizes is embedded in coral-coloured earth to form a lively pattern.

Similarly tucked away in the depths of history is the true purpose of the building: what the ruler intended to achieve with his castle in Apulia remains a mystery. The fact that the entire building is based on the figure eight continues to confuse scientists to this day. They alternately describe this unique architectural landmark as the 'Crown of Apulia' and an 'irritation for science' as it defies every interpretation with a counter-interpretation. The octagonal ground plan was typically used for baptisteries, tombs or mausoleums, but these purposes are not relevant here. And as a defensive building, the castle is too difficult to defend, for although it lies on higher ground, it lacks both a moat and a drawbridge – on the contrary, access was relatively comfortable and open. Is it perhaps an astronomical calendar in stone? After all, Friedrich was interested in the arts and sciences, founded a university in Naples, discussed matters with magicians and philosophers and even had a command of Arabic. Whether the idea for Castel del Monte really does go back to astronomical calculations remains as unclear as the question of whether Friedrich ever set foot inside this perfect building, which is depicted on the reverse of the Italian one-cent coin.

CASTEL DEL MONTE, ANDRIA (APULIA), 1240–CIRCA 1250

27

WESTMINSTER ABBEY, LONDON

William the Conqueror had himself crowned King of England in Westminster Abbey on Christmas Day 1066. Almost two hundred years would pass before the church also became the burial place of the kings of England – and, at the same time, an architectural masterpiece. Henry III decided to rebuild the church in the Gothic style, and thereby set himself a magnificent monument.

Work on the new abbey church in London began in 1245. The architectural models lay on the other side of the English Channel: the new church aimed to rival the French cathedrals of the Gothic age. The king summoned Henry de Reims as architect. Whether or not the first master builder was actually from the town of Reims in northern France is not certain, but he knew the cathedral there well. The triple-naved abbey church of Westminster was built on a cross-shaped ground plan. The east end, the choir, was designed as an ambulatory with radiating chapels in a style similar to that of the French cathedrals. The high window openings were decorated with stone tracery; the walls and ceilings, columns and buttresses were equally elaborate. Since they were so rich in playful forms, this phase of the English Gothic age is described as the 'Decorated Style'.

During the early 16th century, King Henry VII added the crowning touch to the rich ornamentation of the abbey church. He extended the building towards the east by adding a magnificent chapel in the apex of the choir and had the walls decorated with 95 statues of saints. In addition to the numerous sculptures, what impresses most is the ceiling, which is spanned by delicate fan-shaped vaulting, with the individual fields of the palm fronds projecting far into the space. Describing his visit to this 'most magnificent of all burial places', the American writer Washington Irving commented: 'On entering, the eye is astonished by the pomp of architecture, and the elaborate beauty of sculptured detail.' Henry VII was even buried in his chapel – having first decreed how his eternal life on Earth should be secured: 10,000 masses were to be read here for the salvation of his soul. While Henry VII's chapel demonstrates the wealth of forms of the late English Gothic style, the west end of the building is comparatively simple. In any case it would be another two centuries before the west front followed the magnificent chapel. The twin towers flanking the façade were not added until the 18th century.

Westminster Abbey has a long history as a royal burial place: from the Middle Ages until the 20th century, more than two dozen English kings and queens were finally laid to rest here. The monarchs share their resting place with some three thousand famous people, including the composer George Frederick Handel, writers like Charles Dickens and Rudyard Kipling, and the scientists Isaac Newton and Charles Darwin. One of the most-visited graves is that of the Unknown Soldier, which commemorates those who fell in the First World War.

'STONE SEEMS, BY THE CUNNING LABOR OF THE CHISEL, TO HAVE BEEN
ROBBED OF ITS WEIGHT AND DENSITY, SUSPENDED A LOFT, AS IF BY
MAGIC, AND THE FRETTED ROOF ACHIEVED WITH THE WONDERFUL
MINUTENESS AND AIRY SECURITY OF A COBWEB.'

Washington Irving

WESTMINSTER ABBEY, LONDON, BEGUN IN 1245

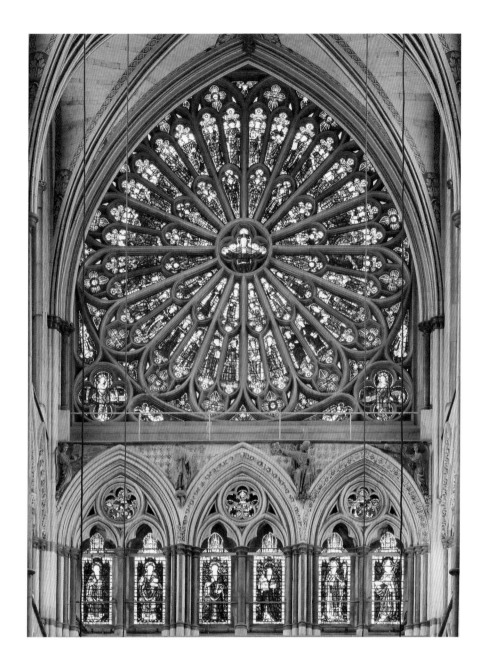

left The new church of Westminster Abbey brought elements of French Gothic architecture to London. The first master builder is thought to have come from Reims, bringing the architectural ideas of the Île-de-France with him. Measuring 32 metres in height, it overshadowed all other English churches although it did not approach the height of the French models that inspired it.

above The design of Westminster Abbey's windows is very ornate. Fine geometric patterns decorate the large surfaces, interspersed with coloured glass. These tracery windows, too, offer evidence of the influence of the Gothic style known from French cathedrals.

WESTMINSTER ABBEY, LONDON, BEGUN IN 1245

28

SAINTE-CHAPELLE, PARIS

Nowadays it is hard to imagine the significance of relics in the Middle Ages. Endless streams of pilgrims travelled through Europe to pray to the mortal remains of saints. The closer the relics were to Mary or to Jesus himself, the holier and more expensive they were. King Louis IX of France (1214–1270) was a great relic enthusiast. It is said that he was given the pillow of St Francis of Assisi as a gift when he was still a child.

In 1239 Louis IX bought Jesus's Crown of Thorns from Baldwin II of Courtenay, his nephew and emperor of the Latin Empire. The Crown of Thorns is of particular significance in the context of the kingdom of France and Louis IX, who regarded himself as an incarnation of the monarchical and religious ideal. As a likeness of Christ, he saw himself as an intermediary between the divine and the human world. He underscored this claim and simultaneously positioned himself as a successor to the suffering Saviour with the acquisition of the Crown of Thorns.

Louis brought the Crown of Thorns to Paris, along with a fragment of the True Cross and the Spear of Longinus, and commissioned the construction of the palace's chapel of Sainte-Chapelle on the Île de la Cité between 1243 and 1248. In accordance with the status of the patron and of the holy relics, the result was one of the most magnificent and 'purest' architectural structures of the entire Gothic period. The lower chapel of the Sainte-Chapelle, which has the appearance of a pedestal from the outside, has unusual proportions: it is 33 metres long, 10.7 metres wide and just 6.6 metres high. To prevent it from looking like a dark crypt, the architect created a six-metre-wide nave with cross-ribbed vaulting and built flying buttresses for the narrow aisles, which are barely recognisable as aisles. He put blind arcades around the walls, which are illuminated by the lavishly decorated tracery windows above.

The upper chapel resembles an oversize reliquary. It is an aisleless church whose walls appear to be made only of glass. The windows are inserted into a framework of rods 12 metres high but only 25 centimetres wide. The thrust of the richly ornamented cross-ribbed vaulting is counteracted by the buttresses on the exterior, which are invisible from the inside, as is the iron anchor behind the frames of the windows. The blind arcades and the sloping windowsills in the pedestal area make the walls appear to be thinner than the 1.5 metres they actually measure. All of these feats of architectural illusionism aim to give the impression of a space of enraptured etherealness. It is like 'sliding from politics to theology', which here takes the form of architecture. The main altar and an elaborate baldachin that covered the shrine with the relics are positioned in the choir. This is because the Sainte-Chapelle was built for the relics. It is the stage upon which the relics were regularly presented until the French Revolution. In order to understand the spiritual value of the relics, it is useful to consider their material value too. The construction of the Sainte-Chapelle cost 40,000 livres, whereas Christ's Crown of Thorns alone cost 135,000 livres. Even during his lifetime Louis IX was considered to be the ideal Christian ruler, and he was canonised in 1297. Like the Crown of Thorns, King Louis the Saint became a relic himself, or to be precise, several relics, which have been preserved here in the Sainte-Chapelle, in Saint-Denis, in Notre-Dame and in many other churches.

THE SAINTE-CHAPELLE, PARIS, 1243–48

The 15 large windows of elaborate stained glass contain 1,113 scenes depicting the history of humankind, from the Creation to the Resurrection of Christ. Fourteen of the stained-glass windows illustrate episodes from the Bible and are intended to be read from left to right and from the bottom up. One of the windows tells the story of the relics of the Passion.

'THE HOTTER IT IS, THE MORE PLENTIFUL THE SPRINGS
ARE AS THEY ARE FED BY SNOW. THIS MIXTURE OF WATER,
SNOW AND FIRE MAKES GRANADA A PARADISE ON EARTH WITH A CLIMATE
THAT IS UNMATCHED ANYWHERE ELSE IN THE WORLD.'

Théophile Gautier

THE ALHAMBRA, GRANADA, BEGUN IN 1238

29

ALHAMBRA, GRANADA

On a hill overlooking the southern Spanish city of Granada stands the imposing palace complex of the Alhambra – 'this petrified dream from the Stories from 1001 Nights'. The palace behind the walls fortified with towers is a gesamtkunstwerk of architecture and landscape art, calligraphy, crafts – and the art of building with water.

The Iberian Peninsula was for almost eight centuries an outpost of Islamic culture and civilisation in Europe. The Alhambra – or Red Palace, to translate the Arabic name – is an impressive monument to Arabic culture in Spanish Andalusia. Depending on the time of day, its powerful brick walls glow in reddish hues. The complex was given its present appearance after the Nasrid dynasty had made Granada its capital city in 1238. The fortress itself, the *alcazaba* in the west, is only one part of the palace complex. The royal palace is at the heart of the ensemble, housing not only the living quarters and rooms in which the ruler held formal receptions, but also the government and administration. With its colourful tiles with geometric patterns, Arabic inscriptions and vegetal ornaments made of plaster, the seat of the Nasrid rulers is richly decorated. The central element of the entire palace city, however, is water, which was brought to the top of the hill from the River Darro by means of a redirected canal. This water is used to irrigate the blossoming gardens and to fill the expansive bathhouses of the Alhambra and of the summer palace on the opposite side. Burbling fountains and large water pools also characterise the three royal courts inside the Alhambra. Dating to the second half of the 14th century, the Court of the Lions is considered to be emblematic of Arabic architecture: 124 marble columns that were once decorated with gold surround the courtyard. At its centre the bowl of a fountain is supported by the stone lions that give the courtyard its name. Four narrow canals run away from the fountain in the direction of the four cardinal points, and from there lead to the main chambers. The Venetian envoy Andrea Navagero reported in the 16th century that water flowed through the entire palace. He was delighted: 'This palace, though it is not very big, is an exquisite building with wonderful gardens and waters, the most beautiful that I have seen in Spain.' By the time that Navagero visited the Alhambra, the Emirate of Granada had long been history. The reconquest of Islamic Andalusia by the Spaniards ended in 1492, when the last emir of Granada capitulated, and the glittering era of Moorish architecture in Spain thus came to an end.

Construction nevertheless continued in later centuries: Emperor Charles V first sojourned in the Alhambra in 1526. He planned to make Granada the seat of the government and ordered a palace to be built on the fortified hill. When the square structure with a round inner courtyard was built, it marked the arrival of the Italian Renaissance in the architectural ensemble of the Alhambra.

A long pool – its calm water reflecting the architecture – forms the centre of the Court of the Myrtles. A colonnade with semicircular arches edges the courtyard at the short ends. The green myrtle bushes that line the long sides contrast with the white of the marble floor.

30

DOGE'S PALACE, VENICE

From the late Middle Ages on, Venice was an important maritime and merchant power and, with a population of more than 100,000 inhabitants, a true metropolis. The city-state was also wealthy: Venice ruled the eastern Mediterranean and positioned itself as the gateway to the Orient. When the foundation stone was laid for a new seat of government in 1340, it was clear that it should reflect this abundance of power.

A magnificent palace complex was built directly on the Canal Grande over the course of the next two hundred years or so. Eventually, three wings would cluster around an inner courtyard. The close connection with Byzantium meant that the Gothic style took a unique turn in Venice, as one can see from the Doge's Palace. The upper storey of the façade facing the lagoon, for example, is ornamented with a lozenge decoration of red and white marble, there is a crown design along the top of the building, and the middle storey opens on the exterior through ogee arches. The government, judiciary and administration were housed in the new Doge's Palace, as were the living quarters of the current doge. Every Sunday afternoon the city's Great Council gathered in the palace and made decisions that governed life in the mercantile metropolis, as well as electing officials, the senate and the Council of Ten. Building a large hall for the assemblies of the Maggior Consiglio, which had grown to a total of 1,600 members, was thus one of the most urgent aspects of this tremendous construction project. Like the entire Doge's Palace, the message conveyed by the Sala del Maggior Consiglio, too, was carefully fine-tuned: the sophisticated iconographic programme of the hall left no doubt as to Venice's power. The maritime republic's status is emphasised throughout the palace by sculptures, reliefs and paintings. The steps to the palace courtyard, for example, known as the Scala dei Giganti, are flanked by two monumental statues of Mars and Neptune. Hewn from rock, the two gods symbolise Venice's power at sea and on land.

The Porta della Carta, completed in 1442, is the main entrance to the Doge's Palace. A Lion of St Mark is positioned above the passageway that lies between the Doge's Palace and the neighbouring St Mark's Basilica. Before the lion kneels Doge Francesco Foscari, who commissioned the construction of the portal. A magnificent window decorated with tracery is set above them, and sculptures and columns ornament the ensemble. The stone decorations are the work of Bartolomeo Bon. The master builder and sculptor did not come up with the name for the Paper Door, however. It actually derives from the supplicants who brought their petitions to the Porta della Carta in earlier times. As they were not allowed to enter the palace, they handed over their papers at the main portal. Another part of the building has a similarly well-chosen name: the Bridge of Sighs on the east side of the palace connects it to the neighbouring building, a prison constructed in the 16th century, which no doubt prompted many a heavy sigh. The infamous chambers directly beneath the palace's lead-covered roof must also have occasioned countless sighs. These prison cells, also known as lead chambers, were supposedly escape-proof, but one of Venice's famous sons – Giacomo Casanova – proved this was not the case when, in 1756, he succeeded in making a spectacular escape.

'ARCHITECTURE IS BASED ON RULES OF BALANCE, PROPORTION AND HARMONY THAT ARE ALWAYS VALID, RULES THAT CAN BE FOUND IN ALL WORKS OF THE PAST: ... THE PALAZZO DUCALE IN VENICE WITH ITS ARTFULLY DECORATED ARCHES, WHICH THE ARCHITECT USED TO CREATE A STRONG CONTRAST TO THE HEAVY WALLS OF THE UPPER STOREYS, IS AN ABSOLUTELY SUCCESSFUL EXAMPLE OF THIS.'

Oscar Niemeyer

THE DOGE'S PALACE, VENICE, 1340–1559

31

MACHU PICCHU, PERU

In 1911 an archaeological expedition led by the American explorer Hiram Bingham travelled through the wild Urubamba Valley in Peru. The group discovered an entire ruined city, overgrown by dense jungle vegetation, three days' march from Cuzco, the old capital of the Inca Empire. Bingham named the place high up in the Andes 'Machu Picchu' – Old Peak.

Around the mid-15th century, the Inca established the large settlement on the rocky plateau at an elevation of approximately 2,300 metres. To this day it is unclear why they chose this col, which is difficult to reach. Only a few pieces of information relating to Machu Picchu are known; the history of the city is shrouded in mystery. According to one legend, the ruler Pachacútec settled there with his entire court and established the cult of the sun god Inti. But whether an Inca ruler ever lived in Machu Picchu is likely to remain uncertain, though it is known that the sun and moon represented the heart of the ritual acts of the Inca. The Intihuatana – which translates as the place in which the sun is tied – was the religious centre of Machu Picchu. A cube-shaped block of stone used as a sun stone by the astronomers and priests of the Inca was located in the sun temple. It could be used to determine the path of the sun, which in turn allowed them to calculate the beginning of spring and autumn. This was important for agriculture. The city built of stone was planned in great detail – and was organised along strict hierarchical lines. The various areas were connected with one another by steps. The temple city was built in the south of the complex, with the royal quarter and the ruler's great palace facing it. Craftsmen and peasants lived in one part of town and scholars lived in another. More than two hundred stone structures have been preserved in Machu Picchu, some of them intact to the height of their gables. All of the rocks used to build the houses and temples came from local quarries. The pieces of rock were cut with a high degree of precision, as a result of which they could be used for construction without the need for mortar. The architecture of the Inca is as impressive as their irrigation technique is sophisticated. The latter made it possible to practise agriculture close to the city: the surrounding land was terraced and filled with soil from the Urubamba Valley. The irrigation system used by the Inca to divert water from the mountains to the terraces and into the city still functions today. The Inca appear to have lived in their enormous city of rock for no more than a few decades. It is even possible that the complex was still in the process of being built when the Spanish conquistadors took possession of the area about one hundred years later. And yet nobody knows why the Inca abandoned their settlement for good in the mid-16th century. Hidden between two mountains, Machu Picchu remained undiscovered, the jungle engulfed it and the city of the Inca fell into a deep sleep that lasted several hundred years.

MACHU PICCHU, PERU, MID-15TH CENTURY

THE FORBIDDEN CITY, BEIJING, 1406–20

32

FORBIDDEN CITY, BEIJING

In the early 15th century an awe-inspiring palace complex was built in Beijing, the capital city of China. The Forbidden City remained the political and religious centre of the empire for almost five hundred years. The ensemble of hundreds of palaces and houses, gardens and administrative buildings is no longer used as the seat of government, but has instead become a visitor attraction.

Four gates at the four cardinal points lead into the Forbidden City, but only the select few were allowed to walk through them. Ordinary people were not permitted to enter, giving rise to the name of the complex. Starting in 1406 the Ming emperor Yongle determined the ground plan of the Forbidden City. After years of preparations, the actual construction period was short, and the city within a city was completed as early as 1420. The Chinese emperors considered themselves to be sons of heaven, so that their residence was not merely the centre of their empire, but also, in accordance with their divine ancestry, the centre of the world. Hundreds of thousands of labourers took just a few years to create hundreds of palaces and pavilions, courtyards and gardens. A total of 8,886 rooms lie behind the ten-metre-high walls that surround the complex. The courtyards are clad with 20 million clay bricks. The main axis, measuring more than seven kilometres in length, runs through the imperial city from south to north, with the Meridian Gate in the south functioning as the main entrance. This is abutted by the government district, to which only ministers, officials and members of the military had access. The Golden Water River meanders through this part of the palace, passing underneath five bridges that stand for the five Confucian virtues: humanity, righteousness, measuredness, wisdom and loyalty. The 800 or so palace buildings are made primarily of wood, which was transported to Beijing from tropical forests. The foundations are made of white marble and the curved roofs are decorated with mythological symbols. The Hall of Supreme Harmony is positioned at the centre of the palace complex, on a three-stepped terrace. Large lion figures guard this enormous hall, whose dimensions by far surpass those of the other architectural structures in the Forbidden City – it covers a surface area of almost 2,500 square metres. The ruler's golden Dragon Throne is located inside the hall, which was the centre of the demonstration of imperial power.

Over the course of the centuries, 24 emperors lived in the Forbidden City. Their living quarters were in the north of the complex. The life of the enormous court that surrounded them, consisting of thousands of aristocrats, was governed by strict etiquette. This determined which path was allowed to be used by whom, and that ministers and eunuchs had to approach the emperor and his wife upon their knees. In 1908 Puyi was enthroned in the Hall of Supreme Harmony at the tender age of two. He would be the last emperor of China. He abdicated in 1912 but continued to live in the Forbidden City for another 12 years, albeit under house arrest. Nowadays the gigantic complex at the heart of Beijing is a museum to which thousands of visitors flock every day.

'THERE ARE SOME WHOM NATURE HAS CREATED LITTLE OF STATURE, BUT WITH A SOUL OF GREATNESS AND A HEART OF SUCH IMMEASURABLE DARING THAT IF THEY DO NOT SET THEMSELVES TO DIFFICULT AND ALMOST IMPOSSIBLE THINGS, AND DO NOT COMPLETE THEM TO THE WONDER OF THOSE WHO BEHOLD, THEY HAVE NO PEACE IN THEIR LIVES. THUS IT WAS WITH FILIPPO DI SER BRUNELLESCO, WHO WAS SMALL IN STATURE [...]'

Giorgio Vasari

FILIPPO BRUNELLESCHI, **THE OSPEDALE DEGLI INNOCENTI, FLORENCE,** BEGUN IN 1419

33

FILIPPO BRUNELLESCHI
OSPEDALE DEGLI INNOCENTI, FLORENCE

The Piazza della Santissima Annunziata in Florence is framed by three loggias that do not reveal the appearance and function of the buildings that lie behind them. The square feels like a theatre, an arena, with the steps of the loggias taking the place of the audience's seating area. The Santissima Annunziata church is situated along the narrow side in the north; the order of Santa Maria dei Servi lies in the west; and in the east is the Ospedale degli Innocenti, a home for abandoned children, which was built by Filippo Brunelleschi between 1419 and 1427 and took in its first foundling in 1445.

The building was commissioned by the wealthy silk weavers' guild, of which Brunelleschi was also a member. Today, the main attraction is Brunelleschi's loggia, which opens onto the square, but behind it lies a complex of buildings grouped around a square inner courtyard and consisting of a church, a hospice and other buildings, including a sort of baby hatch, which was in use until 1875. And yet it is indeed the loggia that is of significance to the development of architecture, because it is in this structure that Brunelleschi breaks with all Gothic traditions and programmatically establishes the beginning of a new architectural era. The loggia, which may not seem remarkable at first glance, is essentially one of the first buildings of the Renaissance.

A new architectural era was ushered in by the nine arcades on Corinthian columns and the flanking bays and fluted Corinthian pilasters. The horizontal alignment with the calm, rhythmical sequence of round-arched arcades takes the place of the verticality of Gothic architecture. In contrast to steep Gothic pillars, the dimensions for these columns are on a human scale and the groin vaulting still to be found in Santa Maria Novella is replaced with evenly rounded pendentive domes. The tondi with representations of swaddled babies by Andrea della Robbia (1487) introduce an element of levity between the arches and the architrave.

Of course Brunelleschi drew on various sources of inspiration. These included the classical architecture of Rome, which he had carefully measured and analysed at length, and the Proto-Renaissance architecture of Florence, including San Miniato al Monte and the baptistery. For a long time, people believed, or wanted to believe, that the latter was a classical temple dedicated to Mars. The pragmatist Brunelleschi developed a new formal language from these influences, which aimed in its detail to govern all architectural work, and which Leon Battista Alberti eventually incorporated into the first modern theory of architecture in his architectural treatise *On the Art of Building*, written in circa 1452.

Although Brunelleschi's loggia is the most important one on this square, the other loggias, which are its immediate successors, are also part of the overall design of the symmetrical square as it was planned by Brunelleschi. The loggia in the west was built by Antonio Sangallo the Elder between 1516 and 1525, and the church was erected in the late 16th century.

FILIPPO BRUNELLESCHI is considered to be not only the father of Renaissance architecture, but also the inventor of central perspective in painting. With his famous, though unfortunately no longer extant, painting in the baptistery he succeeded (almost certainly with the use of mirror projection) in establishing the rules for using central perspective in pictorial representations. In doing so, he created a true likeness of the baptistery, which was perfectly executed in terms of scale and perspective. The first extant painting created according to the rules of central perspective is the *Holy Trinity* in Santa Maria Novella, which was painted by Brunelleschi's friend Masaccio in circa 1425.

34

CATHEDRAL OF SANTA MARIA DEL FIORE, FLORENCE

In 1294 the foundation stone was laid for the new cathedral of Santa Maria del Fiore in Florence. The prestigious project took shape only slowly over the course of the next one hundred years. This was because numerous large construction plans vied for attention in the prosperous city and then, around the middle of the 14th century, a catastrophic plague epidemic put all plans on hold.

After the Black Death, which had killed a third of the population of Florence, had run its course, the construction plans for the cathedral were dusted off again. The influential wool merchants' guild, the Arte della Lana, had taken on the responsibility for building the cathedral, and its plans for the dome that would crown it were far from modest. The classical Pantheon in Rome, which had hitherto been the gold standard of dome construction, was to be surpassed. Building a dome with a crown height of more than 80 metres meant setting out on an untrodden path. The guild identified the architect best suited to the job by holding a competition in 1418. The winner, Filippo Brunelleschi (1377–1446), was an autodidact in the field of architecture, but a goldsmith by training who had already made a name for himself as an architect. The cathedral dome would be the Florentine's architectural masterpiece. To this day it remains the largest dome ever constructed of stone. Brunelleschi built it without a supporting frame as the dome, made of sandstone, tuff and millions of bricks, was able to support itself during every phase of the construction process despite the fact that it weighed an incredible 29,000 tonnes.

How Brunelleschi managed to translate his model into a real-world structure was a mystery to his contemporaries. The construction technique has been researched since then: Brunelleschi constructed the dome from two shells. The inner one is load-bearing, whereas the outer one protects the structure from the effects of the weather. Supports connect the shells and strengthen them. This allowed Brunelleschi to reduce the weight of the dome. And yet several tonnes of building materials every day had to be transported to the height at which they were needed. To this end Brunelleschi invented ox-powered goods lifts that had both a forward and a reverse gear. Approximately 100 workers built the dome in record-breaking time: construction began in 1420, and it was consecrated just 16 years later. A second competition was held for a design for the lantern that would crown the dome, and again Brunelleschi's model was selected. His design was executed, though not completed until 15 years after his death, in 1461,. The Florentine architect was, however, honoured with a burial place in the middle of the cathedral: 'Here lies the body of a man of great inventive spirit, Filippo Brunelleschi of Florence.'

The Italian art historian and writer of histories **GIORGIO VASARI** was the first to speak of the 'rebirth', the *rinascimento*, of the arts. After what he considered to be the dark Middle Ages, painting blossomed once again in the early modern period. The Renaissance began in the prosperous merchant city of Florence in the 15th century. The term 'Renaissance' is now also used for sculpture, architecture, philosophy and literature. Characteristics of the culture of this period include references to classical works, an interest in perspectival representation, and the view of humankind as the pinnacle of Creation.

'WHO COULD BE HARD OR ENVIOUS ENOUGH TO FAIL TO PRAISE PIPPO [BRUNELLESCHI], THE ARCHITECT, ON SEEING HERE SUCH A LARGE STRUCTURE, RISING ABOVE THE SKIES, AMPLE ENOUGH TO COVER WITH ITS SHADOW ALL THE TUSCAN PEOPLE, AND CONSTRUCTED WITHOUT THE AID OF CENTRING OR GREAT QUANTITY OF WOOD?'

Leon Battista Alberti

THE CATHEDRAL OF SANTA MARIA DEL FIORE, FLORENCE, 1294–1436

35

LEON BATTISTA ALBERTI
SANTA MARIA NOVELLA, FLORENCE

When stepping out of the train station in Florence, visitors gaze directly at the flat apsis of the monastery church of Santa Maria Novella. The monastery complex with its eight cloisters and inner courtyards used to extend to what is now the area around the train station. It comes as no surprise, then, that the train station is named after the monastery.

The first mention of the monastery and its church dedicated to Mary dates to 983, at which point the complex still lay outside the city walls. The present church was built starting in 1246 and was the largest Gothic church in Florence. It is not comparable to the classic French cathedrals because the builders followed the much more minimalist construction system of the Cistercians. The Gothic pointed arches of the three-aisled basilica are wide and the aisles are separated from the nave by round arches so high that one almost has the impression of being in a hall church.

And yet Santa Maria Novella is important not for its Gothic elements but, most significantly, for its mounted façade, which was planned by Leon Battista Alberti and executed between 1456 and 1470, probably by Giovanni Bettini. Work on the façade in white and green stone began more than one hundred years earlier, as can be seen from the tomb niches situated underneath pointed arches in the lower section. It is likely that San Miniato al Monte (see page 48) served as a model for this, as well as for Alberti's new upper section of the façade. Alberti supplemented the ground floor with a classical-style central portal and two Corinthian half columns and pillars at the corners of the building. The side portals with their pointed arches and decorative elements still date to the Gothic phase.

Alberti's design for the upper storey was subject to fewer constraints. The triangular gable rests on four green-and-white-striped pilasters above the attic area decorated with geometric square patterns. The monumental volutes above the aisles are an entirely new architectural motif. They connect the attic with the gable and had a powerful influence on architecture until the Baroque period. The three small rosettes, which are ornamented with delicate incrustations (inlays), form an equilateral triangle and correspond to the central Gothic rose window, which Alberti had no choice but to keep.

The ground floor and upper storey are of the same height and have an aspect ratio of 2:1. The theory of proportions is a significant aspect of Alberti's architectural theory, which is based not only on his own observations of classical structures in Rome, but also on the writings of Vitruvius and Pythagoras's teachings on harmonious proportions.

LEON BATTISTA ALBERTI (1404–1472) was one of the most important architects of the Renaissance and is considered to be a founder of modern art theory and architectural theory. His work as a writer included books about sculpture and painting (1435), as well as architecture (1451/85). Alberti modernised the classical language of architecture and developed a theoretical structure according to which buildings that deviated from the rules (and Gothic buildings in particular) were considered unacceptable. In addition to the façade of Santa Maria Novella, he created, amongst other things, the Palazzo Rucellai (1446–58) and Sant'Andrea in Mantua (1472–82).

LEON BATTISTA ALBERTI, **SANTA MARIA NOVELLA, FLORENCE,** FAÇADE 1456–70

'ABOVE THE CITY IS THE KREMLIN,
AND ABOVE THE KREMLIN THERE IS ONLY GOD.'

Russian proverb

THE KREMLIN, MOSCOW, EXTENDED BETWEEN 1485 AND 1516

36

KREMLIN, MOSCOW

Russia's worldly and spiritual powers once coexisted in close proximity to one another, behind an imposing wall. Inside the Kremlin the tsar and the patriarch together decided the fate of the country. Although those days are over, the Kremlin continues to be synonymous with the Russian leadership today.

The Kremlin is an enormous complex in the centre of Moscow and is simultaneously the nucleus of the capital city. The former residence of princes grew on a hill above the city from the mid-12th century onwards, and Moscow developed around it. Ivan III had the area transformed into a fortress city from 1485. The Italian architects he had chosen first dedicated themselves to the defence system: a brick wall more than two kilometres in length surrounds the Kremlin with its virtually triangular footprint and encloses the stately 28 hectares occupied by the city within the city. The enclosing wall is up to 19 metres high and interspersed with 18 towers, each of them unique in its design. The tallest of these, the Trinity Tower on the west side, measures 80 metres in height. The main entrance to the Kremlin is built into it. The Saviour Tower is perhaps the best known of the towers, named for its representation of Jesus. It is part of the east wall, which abuts the neighbouring Red Square. The Arsenal Tower, built on substantial walls on the north corner of the Kremlin, was of great strategic significance: the well in its cellar guaranteed access to water in the event of a siege, and the besieged could leave the Kremlin unharmed through a secret passageway.

A total of five churches lie behind the high brick wall, as well as four palaces and numerous monuments, which are grouped around the squares and roads. Together they form an entire architectural ensemble that has been influenced by countless architectural styles from the Middle Ages until the 20th century. The Grand Kremlin Palace was built in the 19th century in the south-west of the complex. Between this and the newer State Kremlin Palace, built in the 1960s, lies the old residence of the tsars, the Terem Palace with its 11 golden domes, built in 1635/36. Expansive administration and senate buildings spread out to the north. Three churches crowned with golden domes lie in the south half of the complex, and Cathedral Square is at its centre. This is also where the bell tower named Ivan the Great is situated. It measures 81 metres in height and dates to the early 16th century. Set on a stone pedestal between the bell tower and the Kremlin wall is the enormous Tsar Bell, cast in 1735 and weighing more than 200 tonnes. Unfortunately, just two years later, the bell was damaged beyond repair in a fire. For the past half century, visitors have been able to admire the 'miracle bell', which measures 6.5 metres in diameter. The Kremlin is among the largest open-air museums in the world. Only the area surrounding the Russian president's official residence is closed off to the constant stream of tourists.

'IN THE FIRST CLOISTER OF SAN PIETRO IN MONTORIO,
BRAMANTE CONSTRUCTED A ROUND TEMPLE OF TRAVERTINE. ITS HARMONIOUS
PROPORTIONS AND CHARMING LINES MAKE IT MORE
ENCHANTING THAN ANYTHING ELSE ONE COULD IMAGINE ...'

Giorgio Vasari

DONATO BRAMANTE, **THE TEMPIETTO OF SAN PIETRO IN MONTORIO, ROME,** 1503–05

37

DONATO BRAMANTE
TEMPIETTO OF SAN PIETRO IN MONTORIO, ROME

The church of San Pietro in Montorio stands on the Gianicolo, a hill on the right bank of the Tiber. A small temple in the courtyard of the neighbouring monastery speaks volumes about the enthusiasm for classical antiquity that characterised the Renaissance. The building became the epitome of harmony and beauty, and its architect, Donato Bramante, was soon judged to be 'excellent'.

Bramante had arrived in Rome in about 1500, where he studied the classical buildings and written sources in great detail. The chapel in the monastery courtyard of San Pietro in Montorio, one of Bramante's first commissions in the city of popes, reveals the degree to which he incorporated them into his own designs. The architect based the building on a classical temple. It reveals Bramante's ideas about the basic forms of the circle and the square, as well as his ideas on the subject of column placement. The 'Little Temple' – *il Tempietto* – as it was soon known, is built on a round plinth and encircled by steps. Sixteen columns surround the building constructed as a *plan centré* on a circular ground plan. Behind the columns lies the cella, which in turn is decorated with flat pilasters. The decorated entablature is fitted with a balustrade on the upper storey and rests on the surrounding circle of columns. The small temple is surmounted by a dome. Bramante's use of the *plan centré* draws on classical models. Most importantly, however, his Tempietto is the first post-classical building to be based on a cella surrounded by a columned walkway. In ancient Greece this was the most frequently constructed temple form. Bramante's design also extended to the surrounding monastery courtyard, which the architect conceived of as a circular space surrounded by columns. The plan was not executed, and the courtyard was eventually built as a square. This did nothing to diminish the Tempietto's fame, however. The artists of the Renaissance regarded Bramante's *plan centré* as the epitome of harmony and perfect proportions. The Tempietto, by the 'excellent Bramante', was the only modern work included by the architect Andrea Palladio in his seminal publication on classical architecture: 'If one considers, then, [...] that Bramante was the first to reveal good and beautiful architecture that had until then remained in the dark, it seems to me that it is justified to consider his work alongside that of the ancients.' His contemporaries, too, were impressed, and Bramante's reputation as a very talented master builder spread rapidly in Rome. Pope Julius II even commissioned him to carry out the most sprestigious project the city had to offer: the construction of the new St Peter's Basilica (see page 102).

DONATO BRAMANTE was born around 1444 in Fermignano, near Urbino. He worked first as a painter, then began to study architecture in Urbino. In about 1476 he moved to Milan, where he designed buildings, including the Santa Maria delle Grazie church, and reconstructed the Santa Maria presso San Satiro church. When the French conquered Milan in 1499, he left the city and settled in Rome, where he designed the cloister for Santa Maria della Pace and the Tempietto in the monastery of San Pietro in Montorio. Pope Julius II commissioned the master builder to build St Peter's in 1503. As master cathedral builder, Bramante designed the original ground plan for the church as a *plan centré*. He died in Rome in 1514.

'FROM THE DOME OF ST. PETER'S ONE CAN SEE
EVERY NOTABLE OBJECT IN ROME, FROM THE
CASTLE OF ST. ANGELO TO THE COLISEUM.'

Mark Twain

ST PETER'S BASILICA, ROME, 1506–1626

38

ST PETER'S BASILICA, ROME

The list of architects is long – but that comes as no surprise when one considers that St Peter's Basilica in its present incarnation with the square that abuts it has a construction history that spans 150 years. Each pope introduced his own ideas and the architect of his choice for the prestige project, and so a dozen architects succeeded one another, including the greatest artists of their times.

The successive architects could not even agree on the shape of the basilica's ground plan: whatever one architect built, the next wanted to demolish or at least alter. On the subject of the eternal building site, even Michelangelo is believed to have said that the Last Judgement would come to pass before St Peter's was completed.

The foundation stone for the enormous construction project was laid by Julius II in 1506. The art-loving pope commissioned the architect Donato Bramante to design a new church to stand in the place of its predecessor above the grave of St Peter. Bramante's plan featured a gigantic central structure on the footprint of a Greek cross. The pope wanted to raise the considerable funds necessary through the sale of indulgences, which spread across all of Europe. The money raised in this way fell short of the monumental plans, however. Furthermore, the new St Peter's Basilica is considered to have been a catalyst for the Reformation, which in turn caused some of the sources of funds to dry up, so that the construction of the church progressed slowly.

When Bramante died in 1514, large parts of the old church had been removed, but only a small part of the new church had been built. Work was slow over the course of the following decades. Raphael was the next architect, inheriting 'the biggest building site that has ever been seen', as he noted. He was succeeded by Antonio da Sangallo and Baldassare Peruzzi, and the ground plan was changed. In 1546 Michelangelo, who by then was 71 years old, was put in charge. The building site remained enormous, but Michelangelo reduced the original plan, making its execution more manageable. This antagonised the supporters of his predecessor Sangallo – with the result that open arguments and hidden intrigues became a constant component of the difficult working conditions at St Peter's. The church progressed nevertheless, and after Michelangelo's death in 1564 the impressive dome was completed according to his plans. St Peter's was now also a symbol of the Catholic Church weathering the Reformation and becoming powerful once again.

Less than 20 years later, however, Michelangelo's *plan centré* concept, too, had been discarded. Carlo Maderno replaced the extant nave of the old church with a new one. His façade, structured by high columns and topped with a central triangular gable, formed the east end of the building, which was completed in 1612. The church was consecrated in 1626, but the calm that now reigned on Rome's prestigious building site proved short-lived, for by the mid-1600s, a Baroque general concept was taking shape. The architect and urban planner Gian Lorenzo Bernini designed St Peter's Square in front of the cathedral in the form of two overlapping squares framed by colonnades.

above The central dome of St Peter's Basilica was built according to plans designed by Michelangelo. Its dimensions are gigantic, with a diameter of more than 42 metres. The upper section is covered in a mosaic decoration dating to the early 17th century.

right St Peter's Basilica is one of the most famous architectural structures in the Christian world – and one of the largest too. The nave alone measures more than 180 metres. The entire interior is richly ornamented with sculptures, reliefs and mosaics.

ST PETER'S BASILICA, ROME, 1506–1626

39

PALAZZO DELLA CANCELLERIA, ROME

In the early 15th century, Rome was in disrepair. Most of its classical buildings had been destroyed or buried and herdsmen let their cows graze on what had once been the Roman Forum. The city's former population of more than a million inhabitants had shrunk to fewer than 20,000 people. The economic and cultural centres were now in Venice and Florence. Not until the return of the popes from Avignon and the end of the Western Schism in 1417 did gradual reconstruction begin.

The Palazzo della Cancelleria, which was built from 1483 onwards for Cardinal Raffaele Riario, a nephew of Pope Sixtus IV, was a milestone in this development. Although the façade had already been completed in 1495, the rest of the building was not finished until 1510. To this day it remains the seat of the Vatican's papal chancellery (hence the name Cancelleria) and is therefore also part of the Vatican's extraterritorial property.

Whereas the construction of palaces in Florence had already reached its apogee in the 15th century, it had only just begun in Rome. And yet the first of these palaces was already a masterpiece. The Cancelleria has an elongated, three-storey main façade that is one of the clearest and most elegant examples of Renaissance architecture, an effect to which the light travertine, some of which originated from the Colosseum, contributes. To avert the risk of monotony on the long façade, the architect arranged the pilasters in the two upper storeys in rhythmically alternating groups, so that all of them frame either a window or a narrower section of wall. The edges of the building stand out like an avant-corps and visually unify the long façade. The pilasters on the brick façade along the Corso Vittore Emanuele II are evenly spaced.

Two portals in the main façade protrude from the building. The left one was created by Domenico Fontana in 1589 and leads to an expansive courtyard, probably designed by Donato Bramante, which opens up in elegant, two-storey columned arcades. The smaller portal leads to the chapel of San Lorenzo in Damaso, which was incorporated into the palace. It is one of Rome's oldest churches and dates to the 4th century.

The architect of the Cancelleria is, unfortunately, unknown because all documents were destroyed in 1527 during the Sacco di Roma, or Sack of Rome. The Florentine Palazzo Rucellai appears to have served as a model for the Cancelleria, which suggests a design by Leon Battista Alberti, given that he was in close contact with the Vatican and had already begun to plan a far-reaching remodelling of the city with Pope Nicholas V in 1450. Alberti died in 1472, however, so that it is possible that Giovanni Bettini, who had already carried out the work on the façade of Santa Maria Novella (see page 96) and was well acquainted with Alberti's plans, was the architect in charge of the execution.

Whoever the architect may have been, the Cancelleria combines the Florentine elegance of an architect like Alberti with the greatness specific to Roman architecture. It thus became a harbinger of the palaces that would be built in Rome.

According to the Italian writer Pietro Aretino, not only did **CARDINAL RIARIO** spend his own money on the palace, he is reputed to have won a large proportion of the construction costs during a game of dice one night – of all people, from the nephew of the man who succeeded Riario's uncle as pope, Innocent VIII. Riario would not enjoy his palazzo for long, however, as the Cancelleria was confiscated after he was arrested for complicity in a plot against Pope Leo X.

THE PALAZZO DELLA CANCELLERIA, ROME, 1483–1510

40

CHÂTEAU DE CHAMBORD

Even Emperor Charles V liked the château, which he visited in 1539, when the complex was still far from completion. He is said to have described it as 'the pinnacle of that which human art can create'.

The enormous construction project of King Francis I would eventually become one of the largest of the Renaissance, accommodating more than four hundred rooms. There was no dearth of châteaux along the Loire, and yet Chambord stood out for its breathtaking dimensions despite the architectural rivals that surrounded it. The fact that the 'utopia built of stone' was never quite finished in no way diminished its impressive effect.

The young king had a preference for the Italian art and architecture of his time, and so he invited numerous artists from Italy to his court. These included Leonardo da Vinci, who spent the last years of his life there. The year of Leonardo's death, 1519, also marks the beginning of work on Francis's record-breaking château. In the Loire valley, close to the little town of Blois, he commissioned a wall to enclose a park and woodland area measuring 5,500 hectares, on which he built an imposing four-winged complex over the course of the next four decades. The plans are thought to have been conceived by the Italian architect Domenico da Cortona, and Jacques and Denis Sourdeau were also involved in the construction project. The symmetrical ground plan of the French-Italian design is rectangular and laid out around a prominent central structure whose four corners are enclosed by round towers. It is located in the centre of the north side and, like the keeps of mediaeval castles, emphasises the château's fortress-like character. Viewed from the north, the château's main façade is subdivided into three floors. It is more difficult to describe the area above because this consists of a veritable roof landscape made up of chimneys, turrets and decorative elements, oriels, roof pavilions and dormers. The dome over the central staircase tower rises above all of the roofs. The double-helix spiral staircase, 56 metres in height, marks the centre of the château. Winding around three times as it ascends, this architectural element is already visible from afar because of the dome. The spectacular staircase was unsurpassed at the time, and thus a clear symbol of the king's status, and yet the king is said to have spent just 27 days at his Château de Chambord.

In 16th- to 18th-century Europe, the **CONSTRUCTION OF PALACES** was one of the greatest architectural tasks. Monumental dimensions were far from rare during this era of absolutist rulers. The palatial residences, which replaced castles as the seats of the nobility in the 15th century, were often constructed as enclosed complexes around courtyards. Many were open on one side, so that three wings surround a cour d'honneur. Starting in Versailles, this three-winged arrangement conquered all of Europe. The façade is structured through the use of pavilions, often at the corners, and of avant-corps in the centre or on the sides – this being the term used to describe architectural elements that protrude from the building façade.

'IT IS A GREAT THING
WHEN ART SURPASSES NATURE.'
Pierre de Bourdeille, Seigneur de Brantôme

THE CHÂTEAU DE CHAMBORD, BEGUN IN 1519

'THE LOUVRE IS THE BOOK
IN WHICH WE LEARN TO READ.'

Paul Cézanne

THE LOUVRE, PARIS, BEGUN IN THE 12TH CENTURY

41

LOUVRE, PARIS

The building that houses the Mona Lisa and other world-famous art-historical treasures was not always a museum. When it was built in the late 12th century, the Louvre was originally a castle. King Philip II fortified Paris, the biggest city in Europe at the time, and commissioned the construction of the building on the right bank of the Seine. Several centuries later the fortress became the seat of the kings of France.

Its new appearance dates to the reign of King Francis I in the mid-16th century. The king wanted to transform the mediaeval castle complex with its battlements and towers into a modern palace. To this end, he ordered the entire west section to be demolished and commissioned his court architect Pierre Lescot to construct its replacement. The plan called for a four-wing complex with two-storey buildings, but the Parisian master builder was able to complete only parts of the enormous construction project. A section of the square inner courtyard of the Louvre, the Cour Carrée, is all that remains of it. Lescot worked together with the sculptor Jean Goujon, who created the ornate structure, to design the façade with the architectural elements that protruded from it. Goujon populated the upper storey with sculptures that emerge from the wall in high relief. He framed the windows with gables, and the niches next to them house additional sculptures; the wide portals are reminiscent of classical triumphal arches. In the following century the building was greatly expanded. Henry IV had acceded to the throne and wanted to enlarge the Louvre court to four times its original size. These plans finally took shape under his successor. But when the Sun King Louis XIV came to the throne, the Louvre's tenure as the royal residence came to an end. The king chose to pursue another project, the expansion of the Palace of Versailles beyond the city gates (see page 120), and the Louvre was left to its own devices. The royal academies moved into the areas that had already been completed, artists used empty rooms as studios and junk dealers settled in the courtyard. At times, the building was even rumoured to be a brothel.

The fate of the Louvre was decided in the revolutionary year of 1793. The centuries-old building site was turned into the first art museum in France. The architects Charles Percier and Pierre-François-Léonard Fontaine began work on the north wing to provide additional space for the art-historical treasures looted by Napoleon; in Italy alone, the French army carried off almost all of the great collections. Not until the 1980s, however, under President François Mitterrand, was the entire royal palace turned into a house for the arts. One of the oldest museums in the world eventually became the biggest in the world. Since then, about five million visitors a year go on a pilgrimage to see the *Mona Lisa* and the other 50,000 or so art-historical treasures divided among the seven collections. Although only five per cent of the complete collection is actually on view in the 60,000 square metres of exhibition space – the vast majority of works of art lying dormant in depots – the Louvre is among the most visited exhibition spaces in the world.

'ARCHITECTURE HAS,
PERHAPS, NEVER ACHIEVED A
HIGHER DEGREE OF LUXURY.'

Johann Wolfgang von Goethe

ANDREA PALLADIO, **LA ROTONDA, VICENZA,** 1565–69

42

ANDREA PALLADIO
LA ROTONDA, VICENZA

Everybody who was anybody in 16th-century Venice built a villa on the mainland facing the lagoon city. Owning land on terra firma provided more than just an escape from the hectic goings-on in the mercantile town.

The Veneto region to which wealthy residents of the city retreated during the summer months was, more significantly, Venice's granary. That these rural villas were also designed to fulfil agricultural functions is often not visible at first glance. This was in large part the achievement of the architect Andrea Palladio, whose name is closely intertwined with villa culture. The villas of antiquity were the most important source of inspiration for the Italian architect. He also drew on this formal language when he designed his most famous building, the Villa Rotonda. It was commissioned by Canon Paolo Almerico and built on a hill on the edge of the city of Vicenza. The three-storey building owes its name to the round hall that is at its very centre, surmounted by a dome. The ground plan is characterised by the shape of the circle and the square. This was because the architect considered them to be among 'the most beautiful and regular shapes'. He constructed about 20 country villas as symmetrical complexes based on these two basic shapes.

The entrances feature porches that Palladio designed as temple fronts: six Ionic columns support a triangular gable. 'For all villas and some city houses, I positioned the gable (the temple front) on the façade of the front side,' the architect explained, 'so that these gables distinguish the entrance to the house and serve the greatness and glory of the work by elevating the front section of a building over the remaining parts.' For the Rotonda, the architect considered a mere 'temple front' inadequate and set porticos in front of all four sides of the building – so that the perfect symmetry of the building would not be disrupted by the elevation of one side of the building over any of the others.

It was certainly risky to design a private residence along the lines of a *plan centré* as this layout had previously been used only for churches. The influence of Palladio's example would soon spread, however, even to the other side of the Atlantic: American President Thomas Jefferson's plans for Monticello, his country home in Virginia, drew heavily on Palladio's Rotonda. The Renaissance architect's buildings were widely admired from the 17th century onwards, not only in North America, but also in Europe.

Andrea di Piero della Gondola, known as **PALLADIO**, was born in Padua in 1508. He settled in Vicenza after training as a stonemason, and became acquainted with the humanist tradition. He studied classical buildings in Rome and recorded his observations in influential writings. His chief theoretical work, *The Four Books of Architecture*, was published in 1570. Following the remodelling of the Palazzo della Ragione in Vicenza he became a highly sought-after architect in the mid-16th century. More than 80 buildings in the Veneto were constructed according to his plans, ranging from villas to churches and city residences. His most famous buildings, besides the Villa Rotonda, include the churches of San Giorgio Maggiore and Il Redentore in Venice. Palladio died in Vicenza in 1580.

POTALA, LHASA, BEGUN IN 1645

43

POTALA, LHASA

Lhasa, the capital of Tibet, is situated at an elevation of more than 3,500 metres in the Trans-Himalayan mountains. The cityscape is dominated by the intricate architectural ensemble at its heart: the Potala. The various palace and monastery buildings with their gold roofs stand on a cliff at the centre of the city.

The Potala Palace was until 1959 the seat of the Dalai Lama, the spiritual and this-worldly leader of Tibet. The Sanskrit word 'potala' refers to the seat of the Bodhisattva Avalokitesvara; the Dalai Lamas regard themselves as the earthly embodiments of this being striving for enlightenment. The Chinese occupation of Tibet and the chaos of the 1950s have left their traces on the Potala, too, though most of its art-historical treasures have been preserved.

The palace monastery lies on the narrow ridge of the Marpori, or Red Mountain. The Potala rises 100 metres above the city, protected by a wall façade 360 metres in length. It is said that 999 rooms are tucked away inside it, covering a surface area of 130,000 square metres. Its location high up above the city and its enormous proportions make the Potala look like a fortress on the roof of the world.

The complex was built in the second half of the 17th century. The White Palace on the north side of the architectural ensemble constitutes its core. Its foundation stone was laid in 1645 by the fifth Dalai Lama. The building was completed during his lifetime, serving as an administrative building and, initially, also as the residence of the Dalai Lama. The Tsomchen Shar is the biggest room in the whitewashed palace, measuring more than 700 square metres. The new year was celebrated in this assembly hall, and it is also where Dalai Lamas were enthroned.

To its west lies a palace building painted a vibrant red – the true destination of the numerous pilgrims. The Red Palace is decorated with gold roofs and ridge turrets. With its numerous temples, chapels and meditation halls, the palace primarily served spiritual purposes, although the uppermost of the four storeys also housed the Dalai Lama's living quarters. Magnificently designed stupas, Buddhist burial structures that contain the relics of the deceased Dalai Lamas, are arranged in the Lhakhang, the 'House of Divinities'. The most splendid of the stupas in this elongated room is the grave of the person who originally commissioned the construction of the Potala, the fifth Dalai Lama. His reliquary is almost 15 metres high and decorated with thousands of pearls, turquoises, coral and, most notably, gold. The Potala is the symbol of Tibet and is among the most important sites of pilgrimage for Tibetan Buddhists. The name 'Lhasa' translates as 'Place of the Gods'. Buddhists follow several pilgrimage paths that lead them through the city and to its holy sites. Buddhist pilgrims call the stupa of the fifth Dalai Lama a 'unique treasure of our world'.

Sacred architecture in the Buddhist world varies depending on the time of its construction and on its geographical location. **BUDDHIST TEMPLES** are laid out around a centre, where relics are kept. These stupas were originally hill-like structures that were built as monuments to people who had become enlightened. Gradually, entire temple complexes grew up around these repositories for relics. Their figural ornamentation, consisting of reliefs and statues, provides insights into the life of the Buddha. The monumental terraced temple of Borobudur on the Indonesian island of Java is among the largest works of sacred Buddhist architecture.

left and above The Potala Palace, in the Trans-Himalayan mountains, stands guard over Tibet's capital city. The Dalai Lama's winter palace plays a central role in Tibetan Buddhism. Pilgrims can see its golden roofs sparkle from afar as they approach.

POTALA, LHASA, BEGUN IN 1645

44

TAJ MAHAL, AGRA

In 1612 Shah Jahan dutifully married a woman from a respectable family. The family of Ajumand Banu Begam had a lot of influence at the Mughal court. And yet the union appears also to have been a marriage based on love, and the great Mughal gave his wife the title of Mumtaz Mahal, or 'The Chosen One of the Palace'. He was devastated when she died in 1631.

In the years that followed he dedicated himself to the construction of a funerary mosque that would serve as a memorial to his beloved wife. Following an appropriate mourning period, Shah Jahan began work on the tremendous construction project. The Taj Mahal, or 'Crown Palace', is set on the edge of a garden complex in the northern Indian city of Agra. When the building took shape in 1632, Agra was the capital of the Mughal Empire. Shah Jahan had already made a name for himself, having built palaces and gardens in Agra and commissioned architectural structures in other parts of the great empire, which extended as far as present-day Afghanistan. When it came to the Taj Mahal, the ruler thought in monumental dimensions. The mausoleum became one of the most ambitious projects of a ruler who was already a prolific builder. Approximately 20,000 people worked on the Taj Mahal during the 15 or so years that it took to construct it. Shah Jahan summoned the greatest master builders and craftsmen of northern India for this purpose and drew on Asian architectural styles, which he combined with Persian and European architectural traditions. Expansive park grounds with pools surround the building, designed according to highly symmetrical principles on a ground plan in the shape of a square with slanted corners. Precious materials underline the great significance of the building. The mausoleum is made of brilliantly white marble that offsets the entrance portal of red sandstone. The interior is decorated with mosaics of semiprecious stones, sandstone reliefs and marble decorations. The building is surmounted by an onion dome flanked by additional domes and little towers, and narrow minarets rise above the corners of the marble platform measuring 100 by 100 metres. The funerary structure is also a masterpiece of structural engineering: the dome itself is 65 metres high and 28 metres wide, sheltering the funerary chamber at the heart of the building. Not only is the vaulting ambitious, but Shah Jahan's master builders also had to take into account the great numbers of pilgrims who would be drawn to the grave of Mumtaz Mahal. The shah also had precise plans for his own final resting place: a mausoleum built of black marble as an architectural counterpart opposite the Taj Mahal. But there was no time to execute this plan. His son usurped the throne in 1658 and buried him next to his beloved wife in the Taj Mahal. Although he was not able to carry out his last plan, Shah Jahan's prolific construction activities had a profound effect on India's architectural landscape.

MAUSOLEUMS are monumental sepulchral structures, many of which are lavishly decorated. The word derives from the monumental shrine to Mausolus in Asia Minor. Built on a colossal scale, his tomb, the Mausoleum of Halicarnassus, was one of the Seven Wonders of the Ancient World, and gave its name to this type of architectural structure. Mausoleums often consist of two storeys: beneath the hall of remembrance or chapel lies the crypt containing the actual tombs. Mausoleums serve as memorials to the dead, but they also serve a representative function. During the Classicist period in particular, which drew heavily on classical antiquity, the mausoleum as an architectural type underwent a revival.

'THE POPULATION OF THE WORLD IS DIVIDED INTO
TWO CATEGORIES. THOSE WHO HAVE SEEN THE
TAJ MAHAL, AND THE OTHERS.'

Edward Lear

THE TAJ MAHAL, AGRA, INDIA, 1632–48

45

LOUIS LE VAU AND JULES HARDOUIN-MANSART
PALACE OF VERSAILLES

The French ruler Louis XIV is said to have uttered the modest words 'I am the state.' The 'Sun King' also decreed that his residence at Versailles should be built around him, and the royal bedchamber became the very centre of the gesamtkunstwerk in front of the city gates of Paris. Under his rule, the hunting lodge he had inherited became a palatial complex in which every detail celebrated the king.

France was the new European superpower when the 22-year-old acceded to the throne. Louis XIV wanted his residence to strengthen his claim. His father had commissioned a palace to be built in the woodland west of Paris, and this would serve as the Sun King's point of departure. The majestic architectural framework for the no-less-majestic royal household would be built on these grounds under Louis Le Vau and his successor Jules Hardouin-Mansart from 1668 onwards. More than 30,000 workers and all the great artists of the nation spent several decades creating a suitable backdrop for the picture-perfect stage for the ruler. Three roads led up to the palace, which forms the centre of an enormous star-shaped complex. The main view of the three-winged complex is from the east. The façade is staggered in a stage-like manner, and the north and south wings together with the recessed central section frame the cour d'honneur. Audiences and celebrations were held in the great Hall of Mirrors, which constitutes the centre of the building on the first floor facing the gardens.

Over the course of the construction period, which lasted almost five decades, 500 million gold francs were poured into this architectural demonstration of power – and into the surrounding landscape. When construction began, swamplands still bordered the site on all sides. Louis ordered that they be drained – after all, if the state must obey him, so must nature. A rigorously designed garden landscape covering a surface area of more than 800 hectares was created under the supervision of André Le Nôtre. It contained pruned trees, geometrically shaped beds and symmetrical paths that were lined with statues and marble vases. There were, furthermore, specially built canals whose purpose was to power the numerous water features of the bassins and fountains.

In 1682 the king moved his entire court to Versailles. Around 3,000 courtiers lived in the enormous palace with him, in a household governed by strict court etiquette that began with the ritual rising of the king, known as the *lever*. The royal couple's chambers were on the first floor of the central section. A clock decorated with the head of the sun god Apollo is set into the façade above the royal bedchamber. The message was clear: when the king got out of bed in the morning, the sun rose above all of France.

LOUIS LE VAU was born in Paris in 1612. His key work is the Château de Vaux-le-Vicomte, which he designed for the finance minister of Louis XIV, Nicolas Fouquet. Le Vau was also commissioned to reconstruct the Galerie d'Apollon in the Louvre. He was appointed to expand the Palace of Versailles from 1668, where he developed the representational style of Louis XIV. Le Vau died in Paris in 1670.

JULES HARDOUIN-MANSART was born to a French family of architects in Paris in 1646. As the chief architect to the king, he was entrusted with the supervision of construction at Versailles in 1678. The Hall of Mirrors, the Orangery and the parkland palace Grand Trianon, as well as the entire layout of the town of Versailles, were created under his aegis. Mansart's legacy is also visible in Paris in the form of the dome of Les Invalides and the layout of the Place Vendôme. Mansart died in Marly-le-Roi in 1708.

'VERSAILLES! IT IS WONDERFULLY BEAUTIFUL! YOU GAZE AND
STARE AND TRY TO UNDERSTAND THAT IT IS REAL, THAT IT IS ON THE EARTH,
THAT IT IS NOT THE GARDEN OF EDEN ...'

Mark Twain

LOUIS LE VAU AND JULES HARDOUIN-MANSART, **THE PALACE OF VERSAILLES,** BEGUN IN 1668

The cour d'honneur is enclosed on three sides by the building's wings, which are staggered in a stage-like fashion. No sooner had it been completed than the magnificent palace complex's courtyard was imitated throughout Europe.

'NOWHERE IN EUROPE IS ONE LIKELY TO FIND
... THE LIKES OF THE ZWINGER GARDEN, WHICH WAS BUILT SEVERAL
YEARS AGO BEHIND THE PALACE, NEAR AND PARTLY UPON THE FORTRESS.'

Johann Christian Crell, alias Icander

MATTHÄUS DANIEL PÖPPELMANN, **THE ZWINGER, DRESDEN,** 1709–28

46

MATTHÄUS DANIEL PÖPPELMANN
THE ZWINGER, DRESDEN

The Saxon elector Augustus the Strong had a passion for exotic plants from southern countries. He planned a garden with an orangery and terraces within the fortifications in the city of Dresden in order to protect them from the elements during the winter. His court architect Matthäus Daniel Pöppelmann began work on the Zwinger in 1709.

The version that was eventually executed bore only a faint resemblance to the original plans for the garden. After countless expansions, it had developed into a magnificent piece of architecture for celebrations that consisted of pavilions, galleries and fountains. The workers must have begun to redouble their efforts in the spring of 1718 at the latest. This is when it was confirmed that the electoral prince and son of Augustus the Strong would marry the emperor's daughter Maria Josepha of Austria the following year – and the Zwinger was to provide a suitable background for the grand regal event. The elector's will to create was in no way confined to gardens and buildings. Augustus also commissioned the sculptor Balthasar Permoser to create opulent sculptural decorations. Stone nymphs drift through the world of cascades and water pools, while crowns, coats of arms and eagles compete with Olympian gods. The complex had not been completed by the time the festivities were held, only half of the planned architectural structures having been erected. The side facing Theaterplatz, where the Gemäldegalerie is now located, was therefore covered with a monumental façade. In fact, provisional wooden structures were built in place of a number of architectural elements, such as the Bogengalerien (curved galleries) in the west. And yet many contemporaries were enchanted by the Zwinger: 'No dream of paradise could be more pleasant,' as one visitor noted. The wedding celebrations lasted for the entire month of September in the year 1719. After the nuptials were over, the Zwinger, and the treasury, were unfortunately empty. Construction did not continue until 1722, when the wooden galleries were replaced by galleries made of stone and the Glockenspielpavillon in the south was built as a counterpart to the Wallpavillon. In the meantime, Augustus himself had ensured that his collection of treasures – including antiques, minerals and scientific instruments – were moved to the Zwinger. So were the Rüstkammer (Armoury), the Porzellansammlung (Porcelain Collection) and the Gemälde Alter Meister (Old Master Paintings), for which Gottfried Semper built the Gemäldegalerie on the Elbe side in the mid-19th century. The late Baroque magnificence at the heart of Dresden had its share of critics, too, however. Karl Friedrich Schinkel, who as an architect preferred the classical style, dismissed the architectural ensemble as 'a large building made of blocks' that is 'full of an astonishing wealth of shells and flowers in the worst style'. Whether or not one likes the Baroque complex, the Zwinger and its triumphal-arch-style Kronentor gate are undoubtedly an emblem of the city.

MATTHÄUS DANIEL PÖPPEL-MANN was born in the Westfalian town of Herford in 1662, but moved to Dresden at an early age. In 1705 Pöppelmann became court architect to Augustus the Strong, Elector of Saxony and King of Poland, for whose mistress the architect created the Taschenberg-Palais in Dresden between 1705 and 1715. From 1709 to 1722, Pöppelmann built the Zwinger, which was to be integrated into the elector's new palace, which Pöppelmann had also been commissioned to build. He died in Dresden in 1736.

»'MARVELLOUS WAR AND VICTORY ENCAMPMENT
OF THE INCOMPARABLE HERO OF OUR TIME [...]'

Salomon Kleiner

JOHANN LUCAS VON HILDEBRANDT, **THE UPPER BELVEDERE, VIENNA,** 1721–23

47

JOHANN LUCAS VON HILDEBRANDT
THE UPPER BELVEDERE, VIENNA

Vienna had successfully withstood the Turkish siege, which lasted several months until the Ottomans were finally vanquished in 1683. Prince Eugene of Savoy was among the city's liberators. Over the course of the next decades, he would achieve a series of successes in the service of Emperor Leopold I, and would eventually even be elevated to the rank of field marshal.

In addition to military honours, Eugene also collected books, and his great collection is today part of the Austrian National Library. The prince was also a passionate collector of something quite different: palaces. His Ráckeve Castle was built south of Budapest at the beginning of the 18th century, and he also owned a palatial townhouse in Vienna, to which he made numerous far-reaching alterations. And yet this was just the start of his notable career as a property owner. Eugene had already ordered a garden to be laid out on a large property near the city walls of Vienna in the 1690s. In 1714 he commissioned his personal and official architect Johann Lucas von Hildebrandt to build a garden palace. The Lower Belvedere, a Baroque summer residence with living quarters and rooms for entertaining guests, was completed just two years later. When the prince ended his military career five years later, he refocused his attention on the property. A second palace was to be built in the garden behind the Lower Belvedere, which slopes gently upwards. Eugene again entrusted von Hildebrandt with the work. The Upper Belvedere took shape from 1721 onwards in the upper section of the terraced grounds. It is likely that the original plan was for a smaller piece of garden architecture. After three years of construction, however, an impressive pleasure palace had been built. By no stretch of the imagination could it be described as a garden palace. The building consists of several parts. Each of these is of a different height, and each features an individual roof construction, which results in a lively overall impression. The central part of the palace protrudes from the façade and is decorated with sculptures. From the entrance hall on the ground floor, a grand staircase leads up to the Marble Hall, ornamented with frescos and moulding, at the centre of the palace. In contrast to the Lower Belvedere, this new structure was primarily intended to fulfil representative functions: Eugene's library and his art collection, for example, came to be housed here. Both palaces have in the meantime established themselves as museums: they are now home to the Österreichische Galerie Belvedere and its collections ranging from the Middle Ages to contemporary art. The elaborately arranged garden lies between the two palaces, adding the finishing touch to the gesamtkunstwerk of art, architecture and nature.

JOHANN LUCAS VON HILDE-BRANDT was born in Genoa in 1668 to an Austrian father and an Italian mother. After he had trained with Carlo Fontana, one of the leading architects of Rome, Hildebrandt settled in Vienna in 1696. It was here in 1701 that he entered the service of Emperor Leopold I. Hildebrandt built palaces and churches, including the Palais Daun-Kinsky in Vienna and the former Holy Cross Church of the Teutonic Order in Linz (now Priests' Seminary Church). For Prince Eugene of Savoy, he created the garden-palace complex with the Lower Belvedere serving as a garden palace, and the Upper Belvedere palace for formal functions. In the 1730s he collaborated on the Würzburg Residenz, whose chief architect was Balthasar Neumann. Hildebrandt died in Vienna in 1745.

48

GEORGE BÄHR
FRAUENKIRCHE, DRESDEN

The Saxon elector Frederick Augustus I, also known as Augustus the Strong (1670–1733), converted to Catholicism in 1697 in order to become king of Poland, a move that alienated his mostly Protestant Saxon subjects. They were appeased when Augustus promised not only freedom of religion, but also to build a Protestant church at the heart of Dresden, the city of his residence. It would be the largest Protestant church in Germany.

It was to be modelled on the domed church of Santa Maria della Salute in Venice. Master builder George Bähr began to work on the plans in 1722, but the foundation stone was not laid until 1726. Bähr planned the 'squaring of a circle', a square footprint with a circular arrangement of the pillars, to be surmounted by a dome flanked by four corner towers. This resulted in the famous silhouette, which was entirely in keeping with Augustus's idea of Dresden as a gesamtkunstwerk. The steepness of the outer bell dome does not correspond to the interior, which is semicircular and ends at the height of the tholobate. The circular interior with its curved galleries corresponds to an arrangement centred on the sermon typical of Protestant churches.

By 1730, building costs had more than tripled, which threatened to halt construction. In order to keep within the budget, Bähr suggested building a stone dome instead of the costlier wood structure encased in copper. Iron anchor rings were installed around the dome to cope with the estimated 12,000 tonnes of pressure that would be exerted by the vaulting. They stabilised the sandstone and, as a result of Bähr's construction, the load was distributed not only among the four main pillars, but across the entire brickwork too. Bähr died in 1738, shortly before completion of the dome and was not present at its inauguration. With its height of 95 metres, the dome looks monumental yet weightless.

In February 1945 Dresden was destroyed in a series of British and American firebombing raids and the ensuing firestorm. The Frauenkirche, or Church of Our Lady, might have survived if its windows had been bricked up, for it was through the windows that fire entered the church. The sandstone was no match for the heat, and the church collapsed.

What remained was a 5,000-square-metre heap of rubble, which was left untouched as a memorial against war and destruction. 'Archaeological reconstruction' began in 1993, a computer-aided process in which all the surviving stones were restored to their original location. By the time it was completed in 2005, half of the stones used for the reconstruction – financed in part by numerous donations, including contributions from British and American organisations as well as Elizabeth II herself – had once been part of the original church.

GEORGE BÄHR was born on 15 March 1666 in Fürstenwalde. In 1693, after completing his training as a carpenter, he went to Dresden, where he also studied mechanics. He designed a camera obscura and built a mechanical organ. In 1705, though he had no master craftsman's certificate, he was awarded the title of *Ratszimmermeister* (city council master carpenter) of Dresden. His first building was the parish church of Dresden-Loschwitz (1705–08), which had an elongated, octagonal ground plan. This was followed by two churches in the Erzgebirge mountains (Schmiedeberg, 1713–16; Forchheim, 1719–26). He also built and rebuilt various other churches and created designs for houses in Dresden. Bähr began to plan his masterpiece, the Frauenkirche in Dresden, in 1722. When he died in 1738, he was one of the leading Baroque architects of Dresden.

'YES, DRESDEN WAS A WONDERFUL CITY [...] THE SECOND WORLD WAR WIPED IT AWAY IN JUST ONE NIGHT AND WITH JUST ONE MOVEMENT OF THE HAND. ITS INCOMPARABLE BEAUTY HAD BEEN CREATED OVER THE COURSE OF CENTURIES. A FEW HOURS SUFFICED TO CONJURE IT OFF THE FACE OF THE EARTH.

Erich Kästner

GEORGE BÄHR, **THE FRAUENKIRCHE, DRESDEN,** 1726–43

THE RESIDENCE IS AN EXAMPLE OF THE COLLABORATION OF ARTISTS
FROM EUROPE'S CULTURALLY MOST IMPORTANT COUNTRIES,
A 'SYNTHESIS OF EUROPEAN BAROQUE'.

Extract from the UNESCO World Cultural Heritage Commission's declaration

BALTHASAR NEUMANN, **THE WÜRZBURG RESIDENCE,** 1720–44

49

BALTHASAR NEUMANN
RESIDENCE, WÜRZBURG

Staircases played a key part in Baroque palace architecture. They provided a magnificent backdrop against which guests – and, more significantly, the owner – could stage sumptuous arrival, escort and reception ceremonies. The spatial experience is underscored, and heightened, not only by the horizontal, but also by the diagonal and vertical thrust of the stairs.

Balthasar Neumann became an expert in staging staircases, and he created his masterpiece in the Würzburg Residence. In fact the plan had originally provided for two symmetrically positioned staircases, though only the left one was actually built. This was typical of the entire Residence, however. Since construction had begun in 1720 under Prince-Bishop Johann Philipp Franz von Schönborn (1673–1724) there had been not only repeated changes in ownership, but also a succession of new plans, influences and changes by the owners' various favourite architects, among them Maximilian von Welsch, Lucas von Hildebrandt and Germain Boffrand. Neumann's greatest achievement with the Würzburg Residence lies not just in his architecture, but also in his brilliant ability to maintain an overview despite all the external influences and constant changes, and to finally carry out his idea. This is expecially remarkable because he was at the same time also building important churches, fortifications, staircases, bridges – even a glass factory, whose production included the mirrors for the cabinets in the Residence.

The Residence is a symmetrical complex with two wings, each of which features two courtyards. The central corps de logis opens onto the city with a cour d'honneur and onto the garden with a pavilion whose top floor houses the magnificent Imperial Hall.

The Court Chapel is in the south-west section. The oblong space is dominated by the curved walls and the three oval domes, defining elements that imbue the space with movement. In its decoration and the impression it makes, the chapel is the very opposite of the climax of the Residence: the light-filled, bright staircase, whose vaulting measures 18 by 30 metres and has a rise of 5.5 metres. It was unique at the time of its construction, and was further honoured in 1753 by the largest contiguous ceiling fresco by Giovanni Battista Tiepolo.

Neumann was the ideal architect for his clients, the influential and wealthy Schönborn family, who had succumbed to 'construction mania'. He created an elegant synthesis of the influences of Italian, Austrian and French architecture and even surpassed these with his personal Main-Frankish style.

BALTHASAR NEUMANN was born in 1687 in the Bohemian town of Eger (present-day Cheb in the Czech Republic). The son of a cloth manufacturer, he trained as a bell founder and metal caster and as a master gunner and munitions specialist. He later joined the military and studied engineering and architecture. Neumann became the most important German Baroque architect, creating a large number of buildings, including the churches of Vierzehnheiligen (1743–72) and Neresheim (from 1747), as well as several houses in Würzburg. He worked on the Residence until his death on 19 August 1753. His military career, in which he took great pride, was as important to him as his artistic one. It is no coincidence that the fresco painted by Giovanni Battista Tiepolo shows Neumann wearing the uniform of a colonel in the artillery regiment.

left Giovanni Battista Tiepolo's magnificent fresco features an allegorical representation of the classical pantheon and the four continents. The representation of Europe includes portraits of the Prince-Bishop Carl Philipp von Greiffenclau, along with Balthasar Neumann, the Würzburg-based painter Ignaz Roth and Tiepolo's self-portrait with his son Giovanni Domenico.

above When Tiepolo arrived in Würz-burg in 1750 his original commission was simply to decorate the Imperial Hall with paintings. It was clear, how-ever, that he would be invited to decorate the staircase, too, if the fresco in the Imperial Hall pleased the prince-bishop. By 1752 both the ceiling and two seven-metre-high altarpieces in the Hofkirche church had been completed.

'WHAT MORE CAN I SAY OF **THIS RIVER OF MERCY**, WHICH ALREADY
RUNS THROUGH ALL OF EUROPE, WHEN **PILGRIMS** FROM PLACES SUCH
AS PETERSBURG IN RUSSIA, GOTHENBURG IN SWEDEN, FROM AMSTERDAM IN HOLLAND,
FROM COPENHAGEN IN DENMARK, FROM CHRISTIANENBURG IN NORWAY, FROM NÎMES IN FRANCE,
FROM CADIZ IN SPAIN HAVE ALREADY COME HERE? WHAT USE WOULD
THERE BE IN LISTING ALL OF **THE GERMAN PROVINCES**
AND OTHER **NEIGHBOURING KINGDOMS**?'

P. Benno Schröfl, priest of the Wieskirche

DOMINIKUS ZIMMERMANN, **THE WIESKIRCHE, STEINGADEN,** 1745–54

50

DOMINIKUS ZIMMERMANN
THE WIESKIRCHE, STEINGADEN

The official name of the church – Wallfahrtskirche zum Gegeißelten Heiland auf der Wies, or Pilgrimage Church of the Scourged Saviour in the Meadow – does not really suit its cheerful appearance. No wonder, then, that it also known as 'die Wies' ('the meadow', short for Wieskirche, or Meadow Church), for the idea of scourging feels out of place in these light and airy surroundings. The name derives from the processional figure of a scourged Christ that is said to have shed tears and answered prayers in 1738.

The chapel that was built a year later in response to these wonders was soon covered in votive tablets and overrun with pilgrims. In 1745 Dominikus Zimmermann was commissioned by the abbot of the neighbouring abbey of Steingaden to build a new, larger pilgrimage church. The chancel was the first part to be built. The aim was that it should be able to function by itself as a church if the number of pilgrims diminished substantially. But this did not happen. Far from it: approximately one million people continue to visit the church every year. They may not all be pilgrims, but concern about a dwindling number of visitors was clearly unfounded.

Zimmermann positioned an oval rotunda with a straight central area in front of the chancel. The space was built using the double-shell construction method, with the exterior wall giving the impression that it envelops the inner oval space defined by eight pairs of free-standing pillars. They support the flat trompe-l'oeil vaulting that owes its apparent depth to the perspectival painting on the ceiling executed by Dominikus's brother, Johann Baptist. The space is a rotunda, with the longitudinal axis accentuated by the approach to the chancel, and the transverse axis emphasised by the increased distance of the central arcades and the two side altars. The main space – characterised by a bright expansiveness as a result of the radiating arcade, the use of white and the bright ceiling fresco – gives the impression of being a banquet hall. The adjoining chancel, with its darker shades of red and the gold decoration, looks like a treasure chest for the figure of the scourged Saviour.

Consecrated in 1754, the Wieskirche constitutes the pinnacle of late Baroque church architecture. Zimmermann created a magnificent Rococo church filled with light, though the term 'Rococo' in fact refers to a decorative, rather than an architectural, style. It was invented in the elegant palais of Paris as an expression of the gallant, refined, everyday culture of the courtly aristocracy. It became particularly popular through stucco decoration in Bavarian church architecture as this was the most important field of employment for stucco artists such as the Zimmermann brothers. In the Wieskirche, rocaille – from which the Rococo style gets its name – is not merely a decorative element, but also an architectural one, combining all of the structural elements with one another.

DOMINIKUS ZIMMERMANN was born near Wessobrunn in 1685. He trained as a stucco artist and architect. In 1716 he settled in Landshut, serving as its mayor from 1748 to 1753. His first building was the monastery church in Mödingen (1716–25), followed by the monastery church in Schwäbisch Gmünd (1724–38) and the pilgrimage church in Steinhausen (1727–33), also known as the world's most beautiful village church. It was here that he developed his mature and ornate Rococo style. He often collaborated with his brother, Johann Baptist Zimmermann (1680–1758), who was himself a painter, creator of frescos and stucco artist. The Wieskirche is Dominikus Zimmermann's masterpiece. He lived in close proximity to it from 1754 until his death in 1766.

51

CLAUDE-NICOLAS LEDOUX
ROYAL SALTWORKS, ARC-ET-SENANS

In the history of architecture until the end of the 18th century, attention is usually focused on buildings such as temples, churches, castles and palaces as the driving forces behind the development of architecture. Purely functional buildings such as libraries and hospitals, homes and early forms of manufacturing facilities are only very rarely mentioned.

This began to change with the construction of the Royal Saltworks of Arc-et-Senans and the architect who built the complex, Claude-Nicolas Ledoux. In 1771 he was awarded the influential title of Inspector of the Royal Saltworks. Salt production was a royal monopoly and one of the state's main sources of income, but the large kilns used in the process required huge quantities of wood. In the course of an inspection, Ledoux realised that the saltworks in Salins-les-Bains were unprofitable because of the local scarcity of wood. Ledoux suggested that a new saltworks be built 20 kilometres away, in the forest of Chaux. His pragmatic observation that 'it is easier to make water travel than it is to transport a forest, one piece at a time' prompted the construction of a new saltworks in Arc-et-Senans. The saline water was transported to it by a canal. In 1773 Ledoux began to plan the site, which would consist of workshops, administrative buildings, and homes for the workers. He completed the complex in 1779.

The complex is arranged in a semicircular fashion and built in a rustic classicist style. The house of the director is at the centre, with the large saltworks to the left and right. Two buildings belonging to the administration and four residential buildings are laid out in a semicircle around the outside. All were built according to the same plan, with the middle section containing a central communal kitchen built around a large fireplace. The wings featured the residential areas occupied by the workers. The entrance building with its monumental portico and eight Doric columns lies on the longitudinal axis, at the tip of the semicircle. It contains the bakery and washing room, as well as the guardroom and prison. The passage is designed to look like a salt cave.

Ledoux wanted to increase the status of buildings that were regarded as inferior, such as factories, because he believed that a primary purpose of architecture was to ensure the happiness and moral improvement of humanity. He therefore designed such buildings with traditional architectural elements like columns and gables. This did not prevent him, however, from surrounding the complex with a wall for the purposes of better supervising the workers and securing the production sites.

CLAUDE-NICOLAS LEDOUX was born in Dormans in 1736. He began to train as an engraver in 1753 and studied architecture under Jacques-François Blondel. He started his career with designs for smaller churches, palais and manor houses in the countryside. In 1771 he was made Inspector of the Royal Saltworks. He wanted to replace the elegant architecture of the 18th century with the geometric austerity of Classicism. In 1784 he constructed the theatre in Besançon, the first to have an orchestra pit, and planned 50 customs houses in Paris. As a member of the *ancien régime*, he was incarcerated after the revolution. In 1804 he wrote his seminal theory of architecture, in which he demanded that architecture must be useful to the common people. He died in 1806 in Paris.

CLAUDE-NICOLAS LEDOUX, **THE ROYAL SALTWORKS, ARC-ET-SENANS,** 1775–79

THOMAS PRITCHARD, **THE IRON BRIDGE, IRONBRIDGE,** 1777–81

52

THOMAS PRITCHARD
IRON BRIDGE, IRONBRIDGE

Sometimes, the very architectural structures that look unprepossessing to the modern eye were the ones that sowed the seeds for a veritable revolution. One example is a small bridge over the English River Severn, west of Birmingham. The Iron Bridge, which was named after its most significant construction material, is the world's first bridge to be built of cast iron. It is, in other words, the ancestor of all iron bridges and steel structures in the world.

The area around Coalbrookdale in the British county of Shropshire on the banks of the River Severn had long been a centre of iron processing. The area provided not only iron ore, but also all of the other materials needed for smelting, including clay, chalk and wood. In the early 18th century Abraham Darby achieved a breakthrough in the processing of iron when he used coke instead of coal, thereby producing a higher level of purity in the iron. His grandson, Abraham Darby III (1750–1791), successfully continued this business, leading to the creation of an early industrial centre. It had one disadvantage, however: transporting people and materials on ferryboats had become an issue. In 1773 the architect Thomas Pritchard (1723–1777) therefore suggested that an iron bridge should be built.

Iron had hitherto been no more than an auxiliary material in architecture – it was used for tension rods and reinforcements and the like – despite the fact that it combines a high load capacity with low resource consumption. Darby was very enthusiastic about the idea and began to plan a bridge unlike any other. In the absence of experience with this material, Pritchard planned it as though it were a bridge made of wood. It consists of five large arches, one next to the other, spanning 30 metres, with a road passing over the top. A total of 378 tonnes of iron were needed for the construction of all the elements of the bridge, corresponding to approximately one-third of the yearly production of Coalbrookdale. Nowadays we know that a significantly smaller quantity of material would have been sufficient. Production of the iron elements, which were assembled *in situ*, began in 1779. The bridge was opened on New Year's Day in 1781, and soon it was famous the world over. People flocked from near and far to admire it, and a hotel was built to accommodate the new visitors. Similar bridges began to be built everywhere, prompting a significant increase in iron production. Darby had succeeded in providing architecture with a new construction material. The Iron Bridge proved to be the best possible means of advertising this new material, for the entire world could see its advantages and the elegance that it made possible. New production sites followed, and an entire settlement grew around them. It bears the name of its origin: Ironbridge.

In order to build the bridge, the young **ABRAHAM DARBY III** collaborated with the iron producer John Wilkinson (1728–1808), one of the most experienced experts in the field of iron processing. In addition to developing a process for casting and boring canons and machine cylinders, Darby collaborated with James Watt in 1776 to build the first operational steam engine. He became popular for his idea of building a ship made of iron – believed to be impossible. In 1787 the ship travelled along the River Severn. Darby himself received an award for the Iron Bridge in 1788 from the English Society of Arts, as the bridge was also considered a work of art that inspired authors and painters.

'I LIKE TO STAND ASIDE AND LOOK A LONG,
LONG WHILE, UP AT THE DOME;
IT COMFORTS ME SOMEHOW.'

Walt Whitman

WILLIAM THORNTON, **THE CAPITOL, WASHINGTON, DC,** 1793–1823

53

WILLIAM THORNTON
THE CAPITOL, WASHINGTON, DC

Once it had been decided that Washington, DC, would be the capital of the newly-founded United States of America, Congress was in a hurry. The government buildings of the new federal city on the banks of the Potomac River were to be completed within ten years. This applied most urgently to the Capitol building.

For the parliament building, a hill was designated and a name determined: the seat of congress would henceforth be known as the Capitol. This was a reference to ancient Rome. The Roman Capitol, the most important temple in the city and the seat of the senate, was also positioned on a hill. The classical model would be brought to bear not only on the location and formal vocabulary; the United States also wanted to draw on Rome's republican tradition. The influential politician Thomas Jefferson was responsible for the architectural elements, and even provided the first designs for the structure. In 1793 President George Washington laid the foundation stone for the new building. As the building gradually progressed, so did the layout of the city of Washington. The plans for the Capitol were drawn up by William Thornton, who looked to Jefferson's architectural models and made references to classical architectural forms in his design. Construction began, but British troops destroyed the shell of the building during the British-American war in 1814. The reconstruction work was carried out by the architect Benjamin Henry Latrobe. In 1819 Congress finally moved to its new Capitol, a domed structure with porticos in front of the entrance façades in the east and west. When construction began, the plan was for a parliament building large enough to accommodate the representatives of the 13 founding states. The United States had grown in the meantime, however, and the Capitol soon became too small. In 1850 a competition for its expansion was put out to tender. The annexes built during the next years transformed the seat of parliament into a monumental structure measuring almost 230 metres in length. Two more additions were built for the Senate and the House of Representatives, which in the form of a north and a south wing flank the central circular building. The appearance of the dome, too, was altered by 4,000 tonnes of cast iron. Since 1865 it has jutted up above the east end of Washington's National Mall, the park that connects the Capitol to the president's residence. Its elevated position, the monumental dimensions and the classical organisation of the façade underscore the Capitol's political significance. For many years, the Supreme Court heard cases in the Capitol. The judiciary did not receive its own quarters until 1935. The representatives, whose numbers have grown to 435, and the 100 senators now have the Capitol to themselves.

WILLIAM THORNTON was born in 1759 on the island of Tortola, one of the British Virgin Islands. He studied medicine, pharmacy and art in Edinburgh and London and emigrated to the USA as a physician in 1787. He first settled in Philadelphia and, a self-taught architect, designed his first buildings in the Palladian style, including the Library Company. Four years later he won the architecture competition for the construction of the Capitol, which would become his greatest work. Thornton also built private residences, such as the Octagon House and Tudor Place in the American capital. He died in 1828 in Washington, DC.

54

KARL FRIEDRICH SCHINKEL
ALTES MUSEUM, BERLIN

The development of artistic styles generally progresses from the simple to the complicated, from the clear to the playful. And it is usually the case that an artistic style prompts the development of a counter-movement once it has reached its most complex phase. The counter-movement itself then aims for simplicity and clarity. For example, the Baroque style and the complex splendour of its late Rococo incarnation in the form of the Wieskirche (see page 134) could not be surpassed.

Forms were reduced and the focus was shifted to 'noble simplicity and quiet greatness', which were considered in the early 19th century to be the virtues of classical Greco-Roman architecture. The result was Classicism, which returned to these very virtues at the turn of the century.

Karl Friedrich Schinkel was a protagonist of this new architectural style based on classical ideals. One of his key works is in every respect exemplary of the architecture and meaning of Classicism: the Altes Museum, built between 1822 and 1830 on Berlin's Museumsinsel (Museum Island). Frederick William III commissioned its construction as an architectural counterpart in the pleasure garden to the (now demolished) palace. As a museum, its purpose was to make the royal art collection accessible to the public.

'Frederick William III established the museum in 1828 for the study of all types of antiquities and of the liberal arts' reads the Latin inscription on the entablature above the main façade, which consists of a widely spaced atrium with 18 colossal Ionic columns. A flight of steps leads to the entrance area with another row of columns leading to the two-storey staircase.

Inside lies the square central building with courtyards to the left and right of it. The central building features the greatest surprise offered by the Altes Museum, invisible from the outside: a two-storey rotunda with a dome. Though it is less than half its size, it is intended to be reminiscent of the Pantheon in Rome (see page 22). A ring of 20 Corinthian columns supports the upper gallery, whose walls feature niches for sculptures. This rotunda, like the great building upon which it is based, is illuminated by an opening at its highest point, though this has been closed.

Schinkel's museum building, which rests on three thousand pinewood posts, derives its power from the clarity inherent in Classicism, though it does not lack a degree of sumptuousness and monumentality. The Altes Museum (Old Museum) was one of the earliest museums to be open to the public. Formerly called Königliches Museum (Royal Museum), it was given its present name after Friedrich August Stüler built the Neues Museum (New Museum) between 1843 and 1855.

Born in 1781, **KARL FRIEDRICH SCHINKEL** became one of the greatest German architects of the 19th century. He also worked as a painter and stage designer. After completing his studies in Berlin he travelled through Italy, France and Germany from 1803 to 1805. He worked as a painter of panoramas, romantic landscapes with Gothic churches and as a stage designer for a total of 42 productions, the most famous of which was the stage design he created for Mozart's *Magic Flute* in 1816. His architectural masterpieces were built in Berlin in the classicist style between 1816 and 1830. Examples include the Neue Wache and the Schauspielhaus. His extensive oeuvre remained influential for a long time. He died in 1841 in Berlin after several strokes and a long period of ill health.

KARL FRIEDRICH SCHINKEL, **THE ALTES MUSEUM, BERLIN,** 1822–30

PAUL ABADIE, **THE SACRÉ-CŒUR BASILICA, PARIS,** 1875–1914

55

PAUL ABADIE
SACRÉ-CŒUR BASILICA, PARIS

Two architectural structures in late-19th-century Paris were particularly controversial. The first of these was the Eiffel Tower (see page 158), which was eventually constructed on the Champ de Mars in the space of just two years. The history of the other's construction was considerably longer. Work on the Sacré-Cœur church on the hill of Montmartre began in 1875 but took almost four decades to complete.

The desire for a pilgrimage church arose among French Catholics during the Franco–German War of 1870/71. The plan began to take shape after the end of the war, and the archbishop of Paris was in favour of the construction of an entirely new building. A construction site was chosen on Montmartre in the 18th *arrondissement* in August 1872. A group of Catholic activists began to drum up donations, which soon arrived from all over France. When the French National Assembly decided to support the project, a competition was tendered for the construction of the Church of the Sacred Heart. A total of 68 entries was received, and the one submitted by architect Paul Abadie was finally selected. Until then most of his work had involved the restoration of Romanesque churches, and he was enthusiastic about historical construction styles. He described his design for the Sacré-Cœur expiatory church as Romanesque-Byzantine. The construction type is therefore based on the cross-in-square church in the Byzantine style, and the mosaic decorations on the interior, too, draw on Byzantine models. The main dome is 55 metres high and is surrounded by a further four domes. But 25 years would pass before the central dome was closed, because the funds needed to pursue the ambitious construction project ran out just three years after work on it began. In 1884 Abadie died, and a succession of six architects took charge of the project over the course of the following three decades.

The hurdles they faced went beyond financial difficulties. Opponents of the church regarded the basilica as a 'challenge to the perception of the civic and free-thinking city' and as an attack on the republic. In the meantime, construction on Montmartre continued. In 1900 the main dome was closed, and in 1914 the building was finished. The church was finally consecrated after the First World War in 1919.

Situated on the highest hill of Paris, the monumental church is visible from afar. Its brilliant white colour is the result of the use of travertine stone, which gradually releases its calcite. The church therefore became ever whiter as time passed. Like the Eiffel Tower, the Sacré-Cœur is intrinsic to the cityscape of Paris, and although both structures were initially the subject of controversy, they soon became symbols of the city.

PAUL ABADIE was born in Paris in 1812, the son of an architect. He studied at Paris's École des Beaux-Arts as a student of the architect Jules Leclerc, among others. Church construction was the focus of Abadie's professional interest. In 1844 he became a member of the commission for historic architectural monuments, and the architect contributed to the restoration of Notre-Dame in Paris the following year. Abadie became a member of the commission for church art and church construction in 1849, and in the years that followed held the office of diocesan architect in various dioceses, including that of the French capital from 1874 onwards. His church designs drew on historicist ideas. Abadie died in Chatou in 1884.

'BUT SEE, WHERE THE MOONLIGHT
YONDER GLEAMS,
A FORM OF MONSTROUS SORT IT IS!
AS BLACK AS THE DEVIL IT REARS ITS HEAD
COLOGNE CATHEDRAL IN SHORT 'TIS'

Heinrich Heine, *A Winter's Tale*, 1844

COLOGNE CATHEDRAL, BEGUN IN 1248

56

COLOGNE CATHEDRAL

As has often been the case in the history of architecture, relics were the real reason for radical reconstruction in Cologne. In this case, they were the relics of the Three Kings, which Rainald von Dassel looted in Milan in 1164 and brought to Cologne. One could say that they were among the Top Ten of the mediaeval cult of relics, and became a source of great fame and even greater riches for the city of Cologne.

The Three Kings Shrine by Nicolas de Verdun (circa 1180–1230), built to house the relics, became one of the most magnificent reliquaries of the Middle Ages. The Carolingian-Ottonian building that preceded it was much too small to provide an adequate stage and to cope with the floods of pilgrims.

Work on the new building began in 1248, and the intention was initially to demolish and rebuild only the chancel, but in the process the whole cathedral burned to the ground. This made it possible to think in entirely new – and enormous – dimensions, in accordance with the needs of the diocese of Cologne and of the relics. Both the Constantinian St Peter's Basilica in Rome and the modern cathedrals of the Île-de-France served as models.

Plans were drawn up for a five-aisled basilica with a three-aisled transept and a five-aisled ambulatory with seven radial chapels. In 1322 the colossal and simultaneously delicate chancel was consecrated. Construction was delayed after that because of protests by the population, and so the construction of the façade did not begin until 1350. Like the rest of the cathedral, this remained a torso, however, as both money and interest in the cathedral and its completion waned over the course of the centuries. In circa 1530 all work was halted. At this point the chancel, the southern nave and the beginnings of the south tower had been built. A crane perched upon the tower and would remain the symbol of the city of Cologne for the next three hundred years.

In 1814 and 1816 the architect Georg Moller (1784–1852) and the art historian Sulpiz Boisserée (1783–1854) made sensational discoveries: they found the original parchment plan, more than four metres in length, which had been drawn in circa 1300 by either the first and brilliant master builder, Master Gerhard, or by Master Arnold, one of his successors. This became the basis for the continued construction.

In order to heighten enthusiasm, Boisserée published sections and details of the cathedral as if they were of a completed architectural structure. And he was successful, for in 1842 the foundation stone for the continued construction was laid. Most of the funding was provided by Emperor Frederick William IV and the Prussian state, the Zentral-Dombau-Verein (Central Cathedral Building Society) and various cathedral-construction lotteries.

A commission ensured that the mediaeval forms and building techniques were followed. An exception was made for the roof, however, which was constructed using rolled iron, according to the most recent technical advances. It was at the time the largest iron structure in Europe. The cathedral is believed to have survived the aerial bombings of the Second World War thanks to this exception.

Both towers, each measuring more than 156 metres, were completed in 1880. The cathedral remained the tallest building in the world until 1884. According to a local saying, the world will end once Cologne Cathedral has been completed. This may explain why more than 60 craftsmen and artists continue to work on the cathedral.

Cologne Cathedral is the pinnacle of the Gothic architectural style and also one of the most complex architectural undertakings of the 19th century. In terms of structural engineering, it is perfect, and its sky-scraping Gothic upward thrust remains unsurpassed. It is difficult to imagine that its five aisles could easily fit inside St Peter's Basilica in Rome.

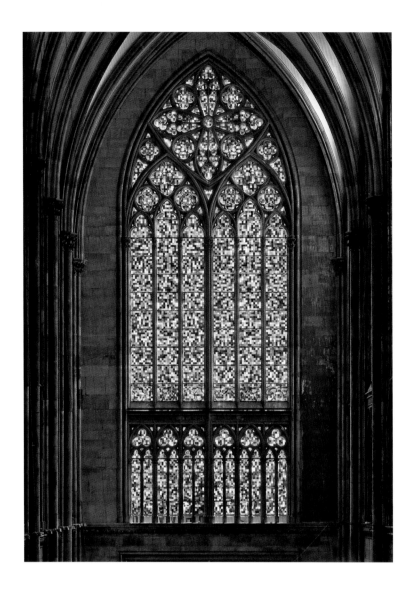

above In 2006 Gerhard Richter was commissioned to design the church window for the south transept. He used 72 colours, which he arranged using a random generator. The surface area of the window (113 square metres) consists of 11,263 squares of colour, each of which is 9.6 square centimetres in size. Richter chose the colours to correspond to those in mediaeval windows and windows from the 19th century.

right A view of the north aisle. Although it was completed in the 19th century the master builders managed to create a seamless transition between the newer parts and the spirit and architecture of the Gothic period. The cathedral's overall length is 144 metres. The nave is almost 44 metres high and just 14 metres wide, and the height of the aisles is less than half that of the nave.

57

ANTONI GAUDÍ
SAGRADA FAMÍLIA, BARCELONA

For more than 130 years, Barcelona's landmark has been a building site. Nobody could claim that it lacks visitors given that thousands of people every day visit the Sagrada Família, which has been in construction since 1882. There, they can experience the incremental progress made by the 20 or so architects and up to 200 workers. Every year, some 20 million euros are spent on the building – a considerable sum of money for the construction of a church.

A group of Catholics initiated the construction of the expiatory church, which they wanted to finance by donations. In 1883 the Catalan architect Antoni Gaudí was commissioned as project manager. Only the crypt of the Church of the Holy Family, the construction of which had begun one year previously on a cross-shaped ground plan, had so far been built. The 31-year-old architect's vision of the scale of the church was far from humble: it would hold 10,000 people, 1,500 singers would sing from the gallery, and the exterior would be characterised by 18 towers. Even at that stage it was clear that it would not be completed quickly: 'My client is not in a hurry,' Gaudí stated, referring not so much to his earthly clients as to God Himself. During the last years of his life, the architect worked on nothing other than the Sagrada Família, and eventually even lived on the building site. And yet that is what he left to posterity: a building site.

Nature was the source of Gaudí's great inspiration: everything already existed in nature if only one knew how to perceive it. The pillars and columns inside the church therefore look like tree trunks upon whose branches stone leaves, flowers and insects abound. Light enters the nave through the openings in the vaulted ceiling as though filtered through a canopy of leaves. Eight of the 18 towers have so far been built. The highest tower at present measures 112 metres and overshadows the surrounding residential area of Eixample. The main showpiece, however, is still missing: a tower measuring 170 metres that will preside over the centre of the church, crowned with a cross made of metal and glass.

When he died – Gaudí was struck by a tram – the Sagrada Família was an enormous building site. The apse had already been built, but of the three main façades only that in the east, featuring a representation of the Birth of Christ, was already under construction. Even here, only one of the four towers had been erected. In total, roughly one-tenth of the structure had been completed, and progress was slow; Gaudí's construction plans were burned during the ravages of the Spanish Civil War (1936–39). It was necessary to reassemble plaster models and carry out calculations on Gaudí's geometry before construction could resume in the decades that followed. Approximately two-thirds of the original plan has been carried out to date. The sixth chief architect to follow Gaudí is currently at work, watching over the construction progress on the Church of the Holy Family, which is financed by entrance fees and donations. Even today, no one is ready to predict the date of completion.

ANTONI GAUDÍ Y CORNET was born in the Catalan town of Reus in 1852 and studied architecture in Barcelona. He left university with mediocre marks, but soon found influential clients. As a young architect, Gaudí built homes for Catalonia's bourgeoisie, drawing on traditions of historical craftsmanship in the style of 'modernisme'. The construction of the Sagrada Família in the centre of Barcelona occupied the architect for more than four decades, and yet the church was still incomplete at the time of his death. Gaudí died in 1926 after an accident and was buried in the crypt of the Sagrada Família.

ANTONI GAUDÍ, **SAGRADA FAMÍLIA, BARCELONA,** BEGUN IN 1882

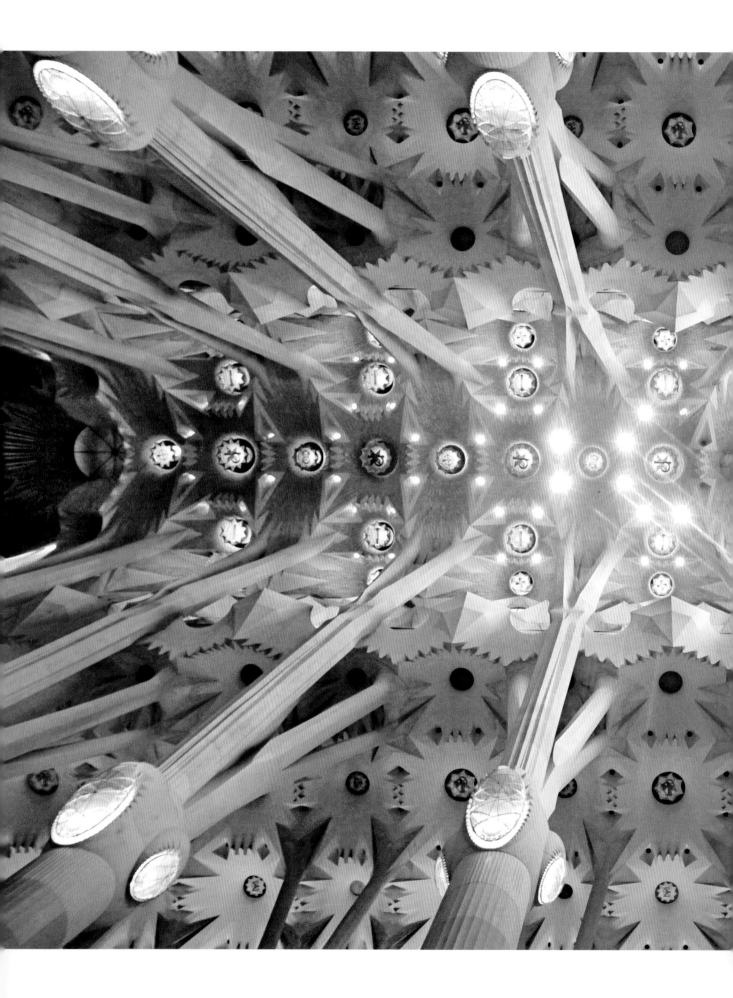

The roof of the Sagrada Família rests on pillars that interlace at lofty heights like the branches of trees. Openings in the ceiling vault allow light to enter the interior as though through a canopy of leaves. Gaudí said that nature herself was his teacher as he built his forest of stone.

58

HORACE JONES AND JOHN WOLFE BARRY
TOWER BRIDGE, LONDON

There are 34 bridges in what is now the London metropolitan area. For a long time, London's only bridge over the Thames was London Bridge, whose origins can be traced to the Romans. The only other way to cross the river was by a ferry or other type of boat. In the early 19th century the economy experienced considerable development. The population increased and more bridges were built, though only to the west of London Bridge.

The port area flourished in the east, which increased the pressure to build a crossing over the Thames here too. People sometimes had to wait for several hours to cross London Bridge, which was closest to the port, because of the high volume of traffic. In 1876 the decision was made to remedy the situation. The Special Bridge or Subway Committee was established to find a solution to the problem by putting it out to tender. The winning entry among the 50 designs submitted was by Horace Jones (1819–1887) and John Wolfe Barry (1836–1918). They planned a combined suspension and bascule bridge 244 metres in length. Its two symmetrical towers are its most remarkable characteristics. The bridge takes its name not from these two towers, which are 65 metres high, but from the Tower of London, located in close proximity to the bridge on the north bank of the Thames (see page 58). Construction of the two massive piers for the towers began in October 1884. They were made of iron cased in granite and limestone and were positioned in the river 61 metres apart. This was done both for practical purposes: to protect them, and for aesthetic reasons: to align them, in town-planning terms, with the Tower. The neo-Gothic Victorian style – also known as 'Gothic Revival', which aimed to eschew all French and Italian influence – was also a symbol of British independence. On the occasion of Queen Elizabeth II's Silver Jubilee in 1977, all visible iron elements on the bridge were painted in Britain's national colours of red, white and blue. Two walkways situated at a height of 43 metres enabled pedestrians to cross the bridge even when the road sections were raised, which occurred 16 times a day in the past. The pedestrian area was closed in 1910, however, only to be made accessible to the public again in 1982 as a tourist attraction.

The two sections of road run nine metres above the water level and can be raised to an angle of 86 degrees within 90 seconds. The accumulators, which used to be powered by steam, are housed in the north tower. This original steam-driven machinery was replaced by an electro-hydraulic system in the mid-1970s.

Although the bridge is an important transportation route, with 40,000 cars crossing it daily, it continues to be raised approximately 1,000 times a year, though only as high as is necessary for the various ships to pass. The raising of both sides of the road to the maximum degree is now reserved for special occasions or honours – such as the funeral in 1965 of Britain's wartime leader and Nobel Prize winner Winston Churchill; in tribute to the British adventurer Francis Chichester, who in 1966–67 sailed single-handed around the globe; and in 2012 as part of celebrations marking Queen Elizabeth II's Diamond Jubilee.

'TWENTY BRIDGES FROM TOWER TO KEW –

WANTED TO KNOW WHAT THE RIVER KNEW,

TWENTY BRIDGES OR TWENTY–TWO,

FOR THEY WERE YOUNG, AND THE THAMES WAS OLD

AND THIS IS THE TALE THAT RIVER TOLD'

Rudyard Kipling

HORACE JONES AND JOHN WOLFE BARRY, **TOWER BRIDGE, LONDON,** 1886–94

'IT WOULD NOT BE UNREASONABLE TO SAY THAT THE
TWO GREATEST WORKS OF ARCHITECTURE IN
NEW YORK ARE THINGS THAT ARE NOT BUILDINGS AT ALL –
CENTRAL PARK AND THE BROOKLYN BRIDGE.'

Paul Goldberger

JOHN ROEBLING, **THE BROOKLYN BRIDGE, NEW YORK,** OPENED IN 1883

59

JOHN ROEBLING
BROOKLYN BRIDGE, NEW YORK

The second half of the 19th century was the golden age of bridge construction. Metal had long since become established as the right material for the job when the German-born American John Roebling perfected a new technique for the construction of suspension bridges. He became one of the most sought-after bridge builders in the United States. His masterpiece, the Brooklyn Bridge, has become a landmark of New York.

Even during these decades of bridge-building superlatives, the construction of the bridge spanning the East River between Brooklyn and Manhattan surpassed everything that had gone before. For a considerable time, the Brooklyn Bridge, with a total length of 1.8 kilometres, was the longest suspension bridge in the world. Two high arches built from stone stand at either end, the formal vocabulary drawing on Gothic architecture. They serve as abutments and mountings for the cables. The steel cables are affixed to these pylons and channel the forces of the bridge's weight into the foundations. The engineer himself had developed the necessary methods: using the air-spinning method, the cables were produced from individual wires on site, where they were routed over the pylons and in this way spun in mid-air. In other words, Roebling produced the steel cables for the construction of big suspension bridges on the spot where they were to be used. This circumvented the hitherto almost insurmountable problem of transporting them. Despite this revolutionary technique, or perhaps precisely because of it, the construction of the Brooklyn Bridge was anything but uncontroversial; during the 14 years needed to build it, more than 30 lives were lost. In addition, there were disagreements related to financing, not to mention the fact that Roebling died at the beginning of construction.

His son Washington finally completed the bridge, and when it was ceremoniously opened in May 1883, most critics fell silent. Since then the Brooklyn Bridge has occupied pride of place as one of the most celebrated and most frequently cited architectural icons of New York. A stroll over the bridge proved a particularly fascinating experience for the American writer Henry Miller: 'Walking back and forth over the Brooklyn Bridge everything became crystal clear to me. Once I cleared the tower and felt myself definitely poised above the river the whole past would click. It held as long as I remained over the water, as long as I looked down into the inky swirl and saw all things upside down. […] The bridge was the harp of death, the strange winged creature without an eye which held me suspended between the two shores.'

JOHN AUGUST ROEBLING was born in Mühlhausen, in Thuringia, in 1806 and studied engineering in Berlin. As a 24-year-old, he emigrated to America with his brother Karl. They settled as farmers in Pennsylvania, but John soon returned to his field of study. He experimented with various cable solutions and in 1849 opened his own factory in order to produce the cables he had invented for the construction of suspension bridges. From this point onwards his fame as a bridge-construction engineer grew steadily. The construction of the Brooklyn Bridge in New York was his biggest project. Roebling died in 1869, before the bridge was completed.

'I LEFT PARIS AND EVEN FRANCE BECAUSE THE EIFFEL TOWER ANNOYED
ME TOO MUCH. NOT ONLY CAN ONE SEE IT FROM EVERYWHERE,
BUT ONE COMES ACROSS IT EVERYWHERE,
MADE OF EVERY KNOWN MATERIAL, PRESENTED IN ALL SHOP WINDOWS,
AN INESCAPABLE AND TORTURING NIGHTMARE.'

Guy de Maupassant

GUSTAVE EIFFEL, **THE EIFFEL TOWER, PARIS,** 1887–89

60

GUSTAVE EIFFEL
EIFFEL TOWER, PARIS

What is now Paris's most famous landmark got off to a rough start. Criticism rained down on the plans for the Eiffel Tower almost as soon as they were made public. Contemporaries were unsparing in their poisonous comments and called the design a 'tragic lamp-post' or a 'horrid column of twisted metal'. Even before construction began, the Eiffel Tower had to withstand spirited opposition.

The great significance of the Paris World's Fair of 1889, which was simultaneously the 100-year anniversary of the French Revolution, was to be underscored by a great structure. The government therefore put a competition out to tender and numerous architects made suggestions for a prestigious monument. The winning idea was in every respect modern: a tower of iron, designed by the engineer Gustave Eiffel. He had already made a name for himself with spectacular iron structures such as train stations and bridges. What was erected in just two years starting in 1887 on the Champ de Mars was a great challenge, however, both for the planner and for the viewer, as would become clear. Four pillars of metal shoot up out of a square footprint before merging to form a tip. In 5,300 drawings Eiffel and his colleagues meticulously prepared the metal structure, which measured more than 300 metres, before assembling 12,000 individual parts into a whole. The detailed preparations would stand them in good stead. Defying all fears to the contrary, the structure was stable: neither the iron framework nor the foundations on the Champ de Mars buckled.

Two platforms would provide tourists with a vantage point, and an observatory and laboratory for weather data were to be installed on the third and highest platform. That, at least, was the plan. But contemporaries decried what they perceived to be a lack of deeper meaning, and declared the material to be entirely unsuitable for a public structure. Artists and intellectuals even signed a letter of protest 'in the name of the underestimated taste of the French, against the erection of the useless and monstrous Eiffel Tower'. Opposition was not limited to public opinion, however, and eventually also affected the budget. Following the complaint of a local resident who feared that the tower might collapse onto his house, Eiffel was ordered by a court to proceed with the building work at his own risk. And at his own expense, which amounted to the stately sum of approximately 6.5 million francs. In return he was granted sole use of the tower for the first 20 years. The entrepreneur's courage soon paid off as the Eiffel Tower began to make a profit the same year of its opening. The critics may not have fallen silent immediately, but the two million people who visited the tower during the World's Fair sent a clear enough message.

GUSTAVE EIFFEL was born in Dijon in 1832. The engineer, architect and entrepreneur built numerous sensational iron constructions. In the 1850s he was occupied primarily with the construction of railway bridges, the first of which was the Passerelle Eiffel over the Garonne at Bordeaux. In 1876 the architect opened his own metalworking workshop in Paris, which also produced parts for the Eiffel Tower. Eiffel built a large number of railway bridges in Europe and South America. He was involved in the construction of the Parisian department store Le Bon Marché, and designed the interior framework for the Statue of Liberty in New York. Eiffel died in Paris in 1923.

61

JOSEPH MARIA OLBRICH
VIENNA SECESSION

At the Viennese Gemeinderat council meeting on 17 November 1897 permission was granted for the 'construction of a provisional exhibition pavilion for the duration of a maximum of ten years'. The foundation stone for the building was laid on 28 April 1898, and just half a year later, on 29 October 1898, it was finished. Clearly no time was to be wasted as it would have to be demolished in just ten years.

The Secession continues to be one of Vienna's most famous buildings. Its driving force were artists of the Vienna Secession gathered around Gustav Klimt, Koloman Moser and Joseph Maria Olbrich, with Olbrich also functioning as the architect of the remarkable building. Modelled on the Munich Secession, at whose centre was Franz von Stuck, the Vienna group was founded in 1897 as a counter-movement to the historicising art of its time. The members of the Secession demanded greater artistic innovation and a more liberated individual approach to artistic creation. Art and all of its emanations should, they believed, be part of everyday culture. This was expressed in the motto 'Ver Sacrum' (Sacred Spring), which aimed to express the blossoming of the new art. It is inscribed on the façade of the Secession building, as is the motto above the portal, which speaks for itself: 'Der Zeit ihre Kunst. Der Kunst ihre Freiheit' (To the age its art. To art its freedom). As an independent exhibition space, the Secession building was part of this programmatic approach. Following vociferous protests against the design, the city of Vienna made available the plot of land on Karlsplatz as this was in any case slated for re-development. The building itself was financed by the artists and their patrons. The Secession building must be viewed in conjunction with its decoration as the artists wanted to combine architecture, painting and sculpture to form a gesamtkunstwerk. The building, shaped by bulky cubes, was the first constructed by the young architect. It features various decorations and is surmounted by a dome surrounded by four short and heavy-set pillars. Laurel leaves as a symbol of victory and immortality dominate the decor of the entire building. The dome alone consists of 3,000 gilded leaves and 700 berries. The gilding of the leaves is hardly lavish, however: gold has merely been applied in three concentric circles to the leaves painted yellow. The bottom of the leaves has been coated with green varnish to heighten the contrast. Every summer, real laurel is planted in the two large mosaic bowls, which are called Oerley Bowls after the artist.

The Vienna Secession was, and remains, an association for contemporary art, which continues to be shown in exhibitions here. Just as they were during the founding period, the exhibitions are still regularly the subject of heated debates.

JOSEPH MARIA OLBRICH was born in 1867 in Troppau, Silesia (now Opava in the Czech Republic). The Austrian studied in Vienna under Otto Wagner, a 'trailblazer for modern architecture' for whom he also worked on Vienna's Stadtbahn public transport system, among other projects, from 1893 onwards. His studies led to him to Italy and North Africa, and in 1897 he became a founding member of the Vienna Secession. His exhibition building occasioned considerable controversy and admiration, and so Olbrich was summoned to Darmstadt by Grand Duke Ernst Ludwig in 1899, where he designed most of the buildings and furnishings for the local colony of artists in the Mathildenhöhe area. Following their completion in 1901 they were presented to the public in the first architecture exhibition of its kind. Olbrich eventually abandoned the floral Jugendstil style for his increasingly rectilineal system. His famous Hochzeitsturm (Wedding Tower) was completed in 1908, the year Olbrich died.

'ROYAL EGYPTIAN TOMB', 'ASSYRIAN PUBLIC CONVENIENCE', 'MAUSOLEUM', 'CREMATORIUM', 'CROSS BETWEEN A GLASSHOUSE AND A FURNACE', 'TEMPLE OF THE ANARCHIC ART MOVEMENT', 'HEAD OF CABBAGE', 'HYBRID BETWEEN A TEMPLE AND A WAREHOUSE', 'TEMPLE FOR TREE FROGS'

Descriptions by contemporary critics

JOSEPH MARIA OLBRICH, **THE VIENNA SECESSION**, 1898

62

DANIEL BURNHAM
FLATIRON BUILDING, NEW YORK

The spectacular new building at the heart of Manhattan would rise to a height of almost 90 metres, adding another tall building to a city in thrall to skyscraper mania. The design for the office building was christened 'Burnham's Folly', but the architect Daniel Burnham soon proved that his plan was by no means just a crazy idea.

At the turn of the 19th to the 20th century, skyscrapers appeared all over the Big Apple. Daniel Burnham was one of the most popular architects of this time. Together with his partner, the engineer John Wellborn Root, he translated this striving for height into stone. The underlying technique, however, was based on steel rather than stone. The traditional solid construction method had been replaced in the late 19th century by skeleton construction. This involves an inner steel skeleton that bears weight and thus makes it possible to build to a great height. 'Burnham's Folly', which was originally also called the Fuller Building after the building contractor, was one of the first tall buildings in New York to be constructed around a steel skeleton. The technological innovation was very well hidden: the architect covered the steel core with a stone façade that provides no indication of what lies behind it but establishes visual references to earlier architectural styles. Decorative elements from Italian and French Renaissance architecture are distributed across the entire façade. Geometric relief ribbons extend across stone tiles, and the façade is embellished with medallions featuring masks and coats of arms, wreaths of leaves made of stone, and decorated columns. Limestone and terracotta tiles cause the 21-storey building to appear much more firmly rooted than one might expect of a building almost 90 metres high. The building made an impression not only with its spectacular height, but with another remarkable element too. The wedge-shaped site on which the office skyscraper was built – between Broadway and Fifth Avenue (at the height of 23rd Street) – suggested the building's original footprint. Burnham designed the building with three corners instead of four, its tip measuring just 1.83 metres in width. After its completion it reminded people of the cast-iron clothes iron (or 'flatiron') in common use at the time, and its new nickname stuck. The Flatiron Building is today the oldest intact skyscraper in Manhattan and its eccentric wedge shape has made it one of the city's landmarks.

DANIEL HUDSON BURNHAM was born in Henderson, New York, in 1846. In 1855 his family moved to Chicago, where, as a young man, Burnham became an apprentice in the architectural practice of Loring & Jenney. In 1873 he joined forces with the engineer John Wellborn Root. Together, they built, amongst other things, the 16-storey Monadnock Building in Chicago: the first large building in the USA to be supported by a steel skeleton. The joint practice of Burnham & Root existed until Root's death in 1891. Burnham's popularity as an architect did not diminish over the course of the following two decades, and more than two hundred buildings were constructed according to his plans before his death in 1912. Burnham died while he was travelling in Heidelberg.

'THE FLATIRON IS TO THE UNITED STATES
WHAT THE PARTHENON WAS TO GREECE.'

Alfred Stieglitz

DANIEL BURNHAM, **THE FLATIRON BUILDING, NEW YORK,** 1902

63

CHARLES RENNIE MACKINTOSH
HILL HOUSE, HELENSBURGH

In circa 1900 just about anything was possible in architecture, as in art. The classical styles were over and done with and the styles that drew on them, such as Classicism and Historicism, had been all but exhausted. The new direction, on which there was also international agreement, was Art Nouveau, or Jugendstil, which could be traced back to the English Arts and Crafts Movement.

The Arts and Crafts Movement was one of the first reactions against the early industrial production of furniture, fabrics and everyday items. The founders William Morris and John Ruskin demanded a stronger awareness of quality, design and individuality in arts and crafts. They aimed for the unification of arts and crafts and a combination of architecture and design. Charles Rennie Mackintosh, who won the competition for the construction of the new Glasgow School of Art in 1896, was one of the movement's most famous protagonists. This building, which he completed during his first phase in 1899, immediately made him famous.

By this time, not only churches and palaces, but also houses were interesting objects in the development of architecture. The rise of the bourgeoisie in the 19th century had expanded the work of architects to include private residences for the wealthy middle classes.

Hill House, which Mackintosh built between 1902 and 1904, is typical of his architectural and interior-design style. The Scottish manor houses of the 15th to the 17th century served as his models. And Hill House is indeed reminiscent of these, though in a modern design. Before Mackintosh started to plan it, however, he observed the daily life of his clients, the publisher Walter Blackie and his family, in order to adapt the design specifically to their needs. The outside of the house may look fairly plain, even unwelcoming, and almost inelegant because of its blue-grey exterior, but it makes quite a different impression on the inside. Here, a combination of functionality and elegance unfolds, revealing itself in every single piece of furniture and furnishing. All of this – the interior design, furniture, wallpaper, fabrics, beds and lamps – was created by Mackintosh and his wife, Margaret MacDonald, who always collaborated with him. One could say that they were the first designers. As is generally the case with Art Nouveau, ornamentation plays an important role: white and pastel-coloured wall surfaces are subdivided in unusual proportions with bright decorations of colour and glass. Narrow metal lines depict stylised flowers, leaves and figures. The combination of natural motifs and austere geometric simplicity would also set the tone for the Vienna Succession and other Art Nouveau and Jugendstil artists.

Born in Glasgow in 1868, **CHARLES RENNIE MACKINTOSH** began to work at the tender age of 16 in an architectural practice and attended the school of arts and crafts. Before long he was awarded prizes for his drawings, including a scholarship to study abroad. He created the Glasgow School of Art and various other buildings between 1897 and 1899. It was also during this period that he made a name for himself as an interior designer with the Willow Tearooms in Glasgow. Between 1907 and 1909 he supplied all designs, also for the furniture, for the library annexe of the art school. This would be his last building project. In later years, he worked mainly as a designer of fabrics. He gained international fame in 1900 when he participated in an exhibition at the Vienna Secession. In 1913 he moved to London, and then to France in 1923. He died in poverty in London in 1928.

'IF YOU WANT A GOLDEN RULE THAT WILL
FIT EVERYTHING, THIS IS IT: HAVE NOTHING IN YOUR HOUSES THAT YOU DO NOT
KNOW TO BE USEFUL OR BELIEVE TO BE BEAUTIFUL.'

William Morris

CHARLES RENNIE MACKINTOSH, **HILL HOUSE, HELENSBURGH,** 1902–04

ISMAIL TRAORE, **THE GREAT MOSQUE OF DJENNÉ, MALI,** CIRCA 1905–07

64

ISMAIL TRAORE
GREAT MOSQUE OF DJENNÉ

Djenné lies on the inland delta of the River Niger, one of West Africa's lifelines. The small town experienced a golden age during the 15th and 16th centuries, when trade expanded rapidly in the region. Caravans laden with precious gold and salt passed through the area on their routes across the Sahara.

Although the economic boom came to an end, the town in Mali remains famous for its architecture to this day. The historic centre consisting of approximately two thousand buildings made from adobe features influences from the Islamic architectural traditions that have shaped the region. At its heart lies the city's landmark, the Great Mosque, whose east side abuts a market. The mosque is not only the most famous building in the town, but also the biggest adobe building in the world. There are building traditions that use adobe the world over. Regions in which woody plants are rare, and timber for construction and stones are hard to come by, frequently employ adobe. Adobe is also easy to use: the cylindrical adobe bricks for the Great Mosque of Djenné were produced without a mould and then dried in the sun. These bricks, known as 'ferey', were used by the architect Ismail Traore between circa 1905 and 1907 to erect the mosque on the site of its predecessor, which is thought to have had its origins in the 12th century. The structure rises above a rectangular footprint. Regular floods transform the town into an island, and so Traore built the mosque on a raised platform. Steps lead up to the main entrances in the south and the north of the building, and the kiblah wall faces Mecca to the east. Structuring the north façade are three rectangular towers, interspersed with tall buttresses, which surround the entire building and support the adobe walls. A small number of narrow windows are distributed over the façades, so that the interior, which accommodates two thousand worshippers, is dark, in accordance with climatic conditions. All corners and edges of the building coated with clay are rounded, another consequence of construction-related considerations: adobe crumbles less readily from rounded corners, even in harsh weather conditions. Bundles of sticks embedded in the walls poke out horizontally at regular intervals along the entire height of the structure. What at first sight appears to be decoration fulfils another purpose: the sticks reinforce the walls and also form a permanent scaffolding for the replastering work, which takes place every year at the beginning of the dry season. A feature of adobe structures is their relatively short lifespans. The Great Mosque, too, retains its shape only because it is continually repaired by hand. As the layer of plaster is largely eroded over the course of the year, it has to be renewed after every rainy season.

The Great Mosque of Djenné is built from adobe bricks, and bundles of sticks protrude from the façade at regular intervals. They reinforce the walls and constitute a framework for the plastering process. Extreme heat and strong rains cause cracks to appear that have to be replastered at least once a year.

'I WARNED THE TWO HONEST MEN WHO STOOD BEFORE ME.
TO NO AVAIL. THEY WERE DETERMINED [...] TO HAND OVER THE BUILDING TO
AN ARTIST WHO HAD BEEN OFFICIALLY STAMPED. I SAID TO THEM:
DO YOU, AS MEN CURRENTLY OF GOOD
STANDING, REALLY WANT TO RUN AFOUL OF
THE POLICE? THEY DID WANT THAT. WHAT I HAD PREDICTED CAME TO PASS.'

Adolf Loos

ADOLF LOOS, **THE LOOSHAUS, VIENNA,** 1909–11

65

ADOLF LOOS
LOOSHAUS, VIENNA

In 1909 the demolition of two buildings resulted in a gap on Michaelerplatz in Vienna. The upscale tailors Goldman & Salatsch planned to fill it by building an exclusive menswear shop. The building was also to house the workshops and tailoring studios, as well as the private apartments of Leopold Goldman. An invitation to submit proposals did not lead to the desired result, and so they hired Alfred Loos.

Adolf Loos's clients certainly understood that the architect's plans would be far from conventional, and even expected to receive some publicity if the design caused a controversy. They can hardly have imagined the whirlwind of outrage that would sweep over the building and its architect, however. In order to understand this scandal, which was one of the fiercest in the history of architecture, one must consider what the architectural environment and Vienna itself were like at the time.

According to an old plan detailing the expansion of Vienna's Imperial Palace, Michaelerplatz was to be 'the view of a main façade of the Imperial Palace and the most important square in all of Vienna'. The neo-Baroque façade was not completed until 1893, but as a result its style matched that of Vienna at this time, which had just undergone the most extensive urban redevelopment with the construction of Ringstrasse. Every single one of the buildings along the magnificent new road was in the neo-Baroque historicist style. They were sumptuously furnished by the likes of the Jugendstil artists of the Vienna Succession (see page 160) around Gustav Klimt (1862–1918).

The work of plastering the façade of the Looshaus was completed in September 1910. From a present-day perspective the building looks plain, even modest, but the residents of Vienna were shocked. Loos, who was 40 years old, made a modernist statement that stood in stark contrast to the buildings in its immediate proximity, and in old Vienna as a whole, during a period characterised by a richly ornamented style. The Viennese could probably have accepted the design of the ground floor, with columns of green marble, but the façade above it was perceived as a slap in the city's face: there was no ornamentation, there were no gables above the windows, no decorations, only white plaster. Loos was the subject of virulent criticism in which the building was described as 'the highest pinnacle of spiritual perversity', as a 'freak of nature' and as 'a monstrosity of a building'. As the façade did not correspond to the authorised plans, construction was halted. In November 1911 Loos defended his building at a meeting attended by more than two thousand people. After highly animated discussions and a façade proposal made by the city itself, it was decided that Loos's façade should be built after all. The 'building without eyebrows' and its architect became trailblazers of Functionalism.

Following his studies in Vienna and Dresden **ADOLF LOOS**, who was born in Brno in 1870, lived in the USA between 1893 and 1896. This had a profound influence on him. Before constructing the building on Michaelerplatz he had made a name for himself with interior designs for shops and coffee houses (Café Museum, 1899). He was also active as a writer, arguing in print that the ornament was no longer appropriate to his day and age. His most famous publication was his 1908 essay *Ornament and Crime*, in which he makes the case for beautiful and functional form. In 1912 Loos founded an architectural school and taught there pro bono. In 1922 he went to Paris. The majority of Loos's designs were for private villas, and he had a profound influence on his successors. He died in Vienna in 1933.

66

WALTER GROPIUS
FAGUS FACTORY, ALFELD

Architects and their ideas and innovations play the most important part in the development of architecture. One should, however, bear in mind the influence of their clients, who often have very distinctive ideas of their own and are in a position to hire or reject a particular architect for the execution of their projects. Time and again, courageous decisions to employ unknown or young architects have proved truly fortuitous.

Carl Benscheidt (1858–1947) was such a client. Before launching himself into the business of producing shoe lasts – for this is what was, and continues to be, produced at the Fagus factory – he was introduced to one of the most advanced industrial plants of its time at a partner company in Boston. In 1910 he designed his own factory in Alfeld with the help of an architect. It was important to Benscheidt that the buildings feature workstations flooded with natural light to reduce the cost of electricity for lighting and to provide a better environment for the workers. Until then, the needs of workers had been of little interest to the owners of industrial plants.

Benscheidt was not entirely convinced by his own plans, however. When he received the application sent in by Walter Gropius, he decided to work with him, even though the young architect had not completed his studies. Perhaps he was also swayed by Gropius's willingness to forego payment if his design was not constructed, and by the fact that the architect's brother-in-law was the district administrator of Alfeld.

Gropius had trained and worked in the office of Peter Behrens (1868–1940), as had, for example, Ludwig Mies van der Rohe and Le Corbusier. Behrens had created a milestone of industrial architecture when he built the AEG turbine hall in Berlin in 1909. Gropius went a significant step further with his factory. He liberated himself of all traditions and reversed the relationship between wall and window. The exterior walls consist entirely of windows, except for the narrow brick columns that lean gently inwards. Gropius not only suspended them freely in front of the ceilings of the three-storey building, but also positioned them around corners, which leaves them free of supports. The edge of the flat roof juts out slightly and is aligned with the protruding floor-to-ceiling windows. The brick avant-corps that forms the entrance feels like a reminiscence of traditional architectural forms.

The glass-and-steel construction and the corners constructed without supports imbue this novel factory building with a lightness that is unprecedented in this type of building. Gropius's first great design was not only innovative, but in many respects revolutionary. The Fagus factory is so timelessly modern that one easily forgets that it was built before the First World War. And it is perhaps significant that one of the first avant-garde buildings of the 20th century is a factory building.

In 1908 **WALTER GROPIUS** (born in Berlin in 1883) joined the office of Peter Behrens, having discontinued his architecture studies in Munich and Berlin. After the Fagus factory, Gropius and Adolf Meyer built a model factory for the 1914 Werkbund exhibition in Cologne, and in 1919 founded the Bauhaus in Weimar, serving as its director until 1928. In 1934 he emigrated to England and in 1937 to the USA, where he founded The Architects Collaborative, Inc. (TAC) in 1946 and was able to implement his philosophy of teamwork. The Harvard Graduate Center (1949/50) and the Pan Am Building (now the MetLife Building) in New York (1952) followed. After the war he designed buildings in Berlin once again, as in the city's Hansaviertel neighbourhood in 1957 and the Gropiusstadt complex starting in 1960. He died in Boston in 1969.

'PALACES MUST BE ERECTED TO LABOUR THAT GIVE THE FACTORY WORKER, THE SLAVE TO MODERN INDUSTRY, NOT ONLY LIGHT, AIR AND HYGIENE, BUT ALSO A SENSE OF THE DIGNITY OF THE GREAT COMMON IDEA THAT DRIVES EVERYTHING.'

Walter Gropius

WALTER GROPIUS, **THE FAGUS FACTORY, ALFELD (LEINE),** 1911

67

PEDER VILHELM JENSEN-KLINT
GRUNDTVIG'S CHURCH, COPENHAGEN

It goes without saying that not all architects were enthralled by the innovation in architecture that Walter Gropius and others had radically advanced – and only a small number of clients showed any enthusiasm for cutting-edge modernism. As a result, some architects repeatedly reverted to an eclectic range of styles – which they then reinterpreted.

Grundtvig's Church in Copenhagen is an excellent example of this. It is a modern church whose design not only makes reference to the Gothic and neo-Gothic style, but also takes into account the tradition of village churches in Denmark.

The competition to build the church was won by the architect Peder Vilhelm Jensen-Klint in 1913, but construction did not begin until 1921 because of delays caused by the First World War. The modern church rises above a traditional three-aisled ground plan. Its reference to the Gothic style in general, and the Nordic Gothic brick style in particular, is plain to see. The consequences of using brick as the construction material are unusually far-reaching. All forms are based on the smallest unit, the simple brick. There are no larger, specially shaped bricks and every element from the top to the bottom is determined by the pale yellow bricks. The architect may have intended this equality of all parts to encompass a religious meaning – going back to to the Danish pastor Nikolai Frederik Severin Grundtvig (1783–1872), after whom the church is named.

The façade, which rises like a monument both to Gothic and Romanesque westworks, is dominated by the contrasts created by the longitudinal ridges. These lend the façade an upward thrust that ends in the ornate crow-stepped gable.

The appearance of the bright interior, too, is defined by the yellow bricks and the remarkable combinations in which they are used. Apart from the chandeliers, also designed by Klint, there is no ornamentation. The overall effect is one of extraordinary clarity of all the architectural elements – an impression that is very rare even in Gothic cathedrals.

A residential area was constructed around the church, in a symmetrical layout centred on the church. It was built between 1924 and 1926, also using brick as the main construction material. The church rises above this ensemble as the focus and undisputed pinnacle. The church was completed in 1940, a decade after Jensen-Klint's death, by his son, Kaare.

PEDER VILHELM JENSEN-KLINT
was born near Mineslyst, Denmark, in 1853. After training as an engineer he initially worked in groyne construction on the Danish coast. He then studied at the Royal Danish Academy of Fine Arts, where he would later be given a teaching position. Having completed his studies, he concentrated mainly on landscape painting. He also engaged in handicraft-related pursuits, very much in the spirit of the English Arts and Crafts Movement. Jensen-Klint did not enter the field of architecture until 1896. In addition to Grundtvig's Church, he built several other churches (Peace Church, Odense, 1918–20), as well as various residential and commercial buildings. He even built a waiting room for a tram stop (Bien, Copenhagen, 1907). Jensen-Klint died in 1930 in Copenhagen.

THE EXTRAORDINARY FORM OF THE FAÇADE, WHICH IS
SOMETIMES REFERRED TO AS AN 'ORGAN FAÇADE',
INSPIRED RESEARCHERS IN GREENLAND TO NAME A MASSIF AFTER
DENMARK'S MOST FAMOUS CHURCH:
GRUNDTVIGSKIRKEN.

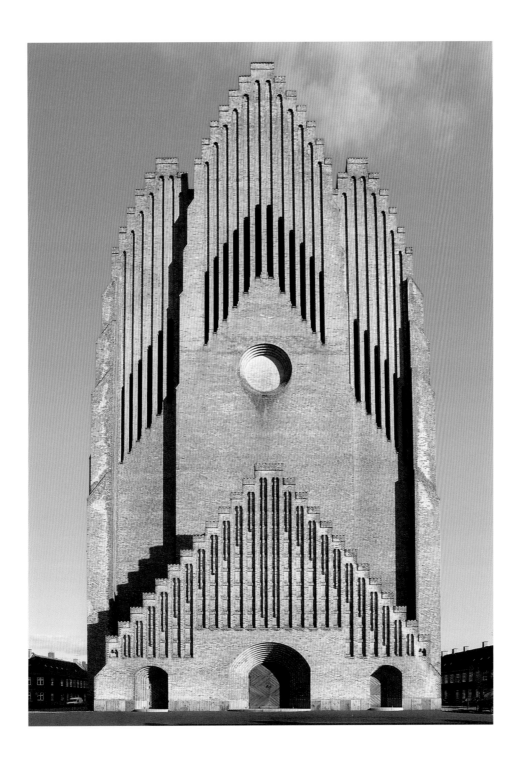

PEDER VILHELM JENSEN-KLINT, **GRUNDTVIG'S CHURCH, COPENHAGEN**, 1921–40

68

FRITZ HÖGER
CHILEHAUS, HAMBURG

There is nothing surprising about an ocean steamer dropping anchor in the Hanseatic port city of Hamburg. Unless, of course, it happens to do so in the middle of the Kontorhaus district – and the steamer in question is made of bricks. So when the architect Fritz Höger decided to build the Chilehaus, he no doubt knew he could expect plenty of attention.

The gigantic office building owes its name to the merchant who commissioned it, Henry Sloman, who had made his fortune in Chile trading in saltpetre. When he returned to the his native Hamburg, the wealthy entrepreneur bought an enormous parcel of land opposite the Speicherstadt warehouse district and handed the 5,000 square metres to the architect of his choice: Fritz Höger. The latter began work in 1922 on what would become an architectural icon in the southern part of Hamburg's old town. Höger used the land – pointed at one end – to build an office building in which no two sides look the same. The height of the structure also varies: depending on one's vantage point, the Chilehaus has between five and eight main floors.

The south side of the building is curved, and the road, which was redesigned at a later date, replicates this curve and thereby emphasises it. The north side, on the other hand, is straight. There are several inner courtyards between the two sides of the building. The ground floor opens up to the street through round arches and verticality is clearly emphasised in the five floors above. Three further storeys are set back, creating the appearance of a ship's railing. These stepped storeys are absent on the east side, however, and the east corner of the building is tapered like the bow of a ship.

Höger's enormous ocean liner with 36,000 square metres of floor space is built of brick, a material for which the architect declared a preference. Almost all of his buildings are clad in brick. Höger felt that brick was like an 'airy veil'. The architect used almost five million pieces of clinker to construct the Chilehaus, and their reddish-brown colour enlivens the façade and forms a contrast to the bright white sash bars of the 2,500 windows. The spectacular east side in particular soon created a stir. Writing in 1923, the *Hamburger Nachrichten* speculated that 'This verticality, which reaches for the sky and finds its grotesque continuation in the protruding corner of the uppermost balcony and roof, will become an architectural landmark of Hamburg.' The newspaper's prediction proved to be accurate.

FRITZ HÖGER was born in Bekenreihe, Holstein, in 1877. The son of a master craftsman, he initially trained as a carpenter. As a 20-year-old, he enrolled at Hamburg's school of building trades, and began to work for an architectural firm two years later. In 1907 Höger became an independent architect who was regarded as self-taught. He co-designed some of the big commercial buildings on Hamburg's Mönckebergstrasse and soon made a name for himself in building Kontorhaus office buildings. In addition to the Chilehaus, which made him famous as an architect, his name is also closely associated with the Kontorhaus Sprinkenhof, which he created together with Hans and Oskar Gerson from 1927 to 1943. Höger died in 1949 in Bad Segeberg.

FRITZ HÖGER, **THE CHILEHAUS, HAMBURG,** 1922–24

'WE HAD TO ARRIVE AT A NEW LANGUAGE FOR THE
FORMS OF ARCHITECTURE, AT NEW LETTERS,
NEW WORDS, NEW SENTENCES.'

Gerrit Rietveld

GERRIT RIETVELD, **THE SCHRÖDER HOUSE, UTRECHT,** 1924

69

GERRIT RIETVELD
SCHRÖDER HOUSE, UTRECHT

One of the most extraordinary buildings of the early 20th century is in a rather inconspicuous location, trapped, as it were, between the end of a row of houses and an overpass across a four-lane urban motorway in Utrecht. The house is exceptional. So, too, were the woman who commissioned its construction and the ideas she realised with the carpenter and architect Gerrit Rietveld in 1924.

When Truus Schröder-Schräder (1889–1985) was widowed, she wanted to begin a new chapter in her life with her three children. She had already designed a room entirely according to her own ideas in collaboration with Gerrit Rietveld in the spacious but conservatively appointed flat in the centre of Utrecht. She now hired him again and together they designed the house as a mirror of her new approach to life.

From the outside, the building is a cube subdivided by Rietveld into different levels of planes and supports. Each one is articulated beyond what is necessary from the point of view of construction, and isolated from the elements that surround it using colour. The planes are white and grey, whereas the supports and rod-shaped sections are in the primary colours of red, blue and yellow, as well as black. With this house, Rietveld, who was part of the De Stijl group of Dutch artists that had formed around Piet Mondrian (1872–1944), could be said to have created a three-dimensional Mondrian painting.

The interior, whose arrangement cannot be guessed by studying the exterior, features additional surprises. There are several utility rooms on the ground floor, but only one on the upper level. This was the wish of Frau Schröder, who wanted to use this area to live in close proximity to her children. In the building permit, Rietveld declared that it was a loft, as permission to build it would not have been granted in the absence of solid interior walls. This resulted in a large, bright room that was designed to provide expansive views. When it was built, the house stood on the outskirts of the city, and plans for a motorway did not yet exist. The large space could, however, be adapted. Schröder and Rietveld came up with the idea of using sliding panels to separate off smaller spaces. The building's dominant motif is the right angle – which was also adopted by the entire De Stijl movement. This was even applied to the windows of the house, which can be opened only at a 90 degree angle. When the urban motorway was built, Rietveld actually wanted to demolish the building. Frau Schröder opposed his idea and lived the rest of her life in the 125-square-metre house. It is now a museum and is included on UNESCO's World Heritage List.

Just how timeless and modern the Schröder House is becomes apparent when one compares it with the design from that period of other ultra-modern goods such as cars, telephones and gramophones.

The trained carpenter **GERRIT RIETVELD** was born in Utrecht in 1888. In 1917 he opened his own business and experimented with new forms for furniture. His most famous piece is the Red-Blue Chair, which he created in 1918. In 1919 he became a member of the Dutch artists' group De Stijl, co-founded in 1917 by Theo van Doesburg (1883–1931). Where painting was concerned the group's aim was the total rejection of illusionistic representation; in architecture it strove for liberation from external constraints on form by means of the interpenetration of surface and support. Rietveld and Frau Schröder built a number of other private homes together. He built four terraced houses for the 1932 Werkbund exhibition in Vienna, and in 1963 he submitted the design for the Van Gogh Museum in Amsterdam. Rietveld died in 1964 in Utrecht.

'FOR THE FIRST TIME, I AM TRANSFERRING THE FUNCTION AND DYNAMIC AS A CONTRASTIVE PAIR TO THE FIELD OF ARCHITECTURE. THIS SCIENTIFIC IDEA DERIVES FROM THE FACT THAT I WAS FREQUENTLY PRESENT WHEN EINSTEIN AND HIS CO-WORKERS WERE ENGAGED IN DISCUSSIONS.'

Erich Mendelsohn

ERICH MENDELSOHN, **THE EINSTEIN TOWER, POTSDAM,** 1920–24

70

ERICH MENDELSOHN
EINSTEIN TOWER, POTSDAM

What might a current-day design look like for a building whose construction was intended to investigate the thesis of a red shift in light predicted in Albert Einstein's theory of general relativity – a building that would use a coelostat to channel rays from cosmic light sources into the building's subterranean laboratories via a 45 degree deflection mirror?

It would probably differ from the plans Erich Mendelsohn used to build the Einstein Tower on Telegrafenberg in Potsdam in 1920. Mendelsohn took an artistic approach to the job of building a solar observatory for the Einstein foundation for spectral-analytical research. The interior organisation of the building was determined by scientific requirements, but Mendelsohn was free to design the exterior as he saw fit. He had become famous in 1919 as a result of an exhibition of Expressionist architectural drawings at Paul Cassirer's well-known Berlin gallery. His designs for the Einstein Tower, which he described as the 'fixing of the contours of a sudden vision', use a solid concrete building as a base. Mendelsohn wanted to create an 'elastic continuity' of the surface and realise in a dynamic form the 'logical expression of movement of the powers inherent in the construction materials of iron and concrete'. He achieved this with remarkable success, but was forced to use brick rather than concrete as the primary material because of the quality of the available concrete and the astronomical cost involved in shuttering the irregular surfaces.

Mendelsohn had to erect the building using a mixed-construction method. The centre, in the form of the tower, was built using the brick construction method and simply plastered. The rim of the dome, the terraces and external walls of the north and south annexes were indeed executed in concrete. The even layers of plaster that were sprayed onto all the individual elements created the impression of a building constructed entirely of concrete. Interestingly enough, Mendelsohn never contradicted the general view expressed in the literature that the building was indeed a concrete structure. The tower was completed in 1922 and inaugurated in 1924 after the installation of the technical equipment.

The building soon began to show signs of severe damage. Water seeped into cracks that had formed, the iron rusted and the concrete was destroyed. The first extensive repairs became necessary in 1927, and these have been repeated at irregular intervals since 1940. The most recent major repairs were carried out between 1997 and 1999, at which point the tower was also given a coat of paint in its original pale ochre.

ERICH MENDELSOHN was born in East Prussia in 1887. He studied in Berlin and Munich from 1907 to 1912. His interests extended from architecture to painting and stage design. He was influenced by Expressionism through his acquaintance with Wassily Kandinsky, Franz Marc and other painters. Most of his designs after the Einstein Tower were for factories and department stores. In 1933 he emigrated to England, and from there to Palestine, where he built hospitals in Jerusalem and Haifa. In 1941 he settled in the USA, where his focus was on the construction of hospitals and buildings for Jewish institutions. Mendelsohn died in 1953 in San Francisco.

71

WALTER GROPIUS
BAUHAUS, DESSAU

In Weimar of the 1920s, children who were being obstinate might well have been told: 'I'll send you to the Bauhaus!' For not everyone in the classically designed little city thought highly of the revolutionary school of art and architecture. When the Bauhaus moved to the industrial city of Dessau in 1925, the local population was more welcoming.

The first task in this new location was the construction of a suitable building. The school for art, architecture, graphic design, crafts, interior design and furniture-making would become a laboratory for all aspects of design. This also meant merging the boundaries between accommodation, work and life. The architect and founding director, Walter Gropius, had a clear ideal in mind: architecture and craftsmanship would coexist as equals alongside industrial production. In their manifesto from 1919, the year the Bauhaus was established, the Bauhaus proponents stated that all members of their crafts school should work together 'without the arrogance that divides the classes and hopes to build a disdainful wall between craftsmen and artists!' To this end, everything would have to be reimagined, from building materials and techniques to living together and working together. And new methods would also need a suitable home.

No sooner said than done. In Dessau, three interconnected L-shaped wings were built. The workshops and the five-storey house in which the residential studios were located stood on either side of a road spanned by a connecting wing large enough to contain an assembly hall and a stage. This area rapidly became the focal point of communal life. Legendary parties, too, were part of the gesamtkunstwerk that was the Bauhaus.

Architecturally, there is not so much as a hint of opulence. One searches in vain for ornamentation or colour. The asymmetrically designed building is undecorated, with most of the façades under the flat roofs made of glass, so that the interior is well lit. A load-bearing steel frame takes the place of walls. The façades of the cubic construction units are varied as their design is suited to their different functions. The workshop, for example, consists of a wall-to-wall glass building. The Dessau Bauhaus, which united all arts-and-crafts-related endeavours under its roof, would soon become the epitome of modern architecture. The school would be of seminal importance from an architectural point of view: cubic construction units, clear, white surfaces and symmetrical rows of windows would define more than just Gropius's buildings in subsequent decades. The 'Bauhaus style' caused a sensation, but the school of art and architecture existed for just 14 years. It was driven out of Dessau after the Nazi party came to power in 1933, and was forced to close its doors shortly thereafter. And yet both the Bauhaus teachers and their architectural ideas had wide-ranging effects, in particular in the USA, after the 'New Bauhaus' was founded in Chicago in 1937.

'LET US DESIRE, IMAGINE, CREATE THE NEW
BUILDING OF THE FUTURE TOGETHER, WHICH WILL
UNITE EVERYTHING IN ONE STRUCTURE:
ARCHITECTURE AND SCULPTURE AND PAINTING ...'

Walter Gropius

WALTER GROPIUS, **THE BAUHAUS, DESSAU,** 1925/26

above The architect Walter Gropius designed the Bauhaus building in 1925/26. The new way of thinking and working was to be expressed in the school building itself, with the architectural structure designed to accommodate the various tasks. Architecture and design, arts and crafts and industrial production coexisted as equals here.

right From the architecture to the ceiling lamps, every detail was designed to be functional. The Bauhaus and its rational designs were to be seminal. The school's training resulted in countless pieces of furniture and objects for everyday use that have long since become design classics.

WALTER GROPIUS, **THE BAUHAUS, DESSAU**, 1925/26

72

LUDWIG MIES VAN DER ROHE
BARCELONA PAVILION

One of Ludwig Mies van der Rohe's most famous sayings is: 'Less is more.' And he arguably never built 'less' than for the pavilion of the German Reich, constructed at the World's Fair in Barcelona in 1929. The pavilion, which was an official commission by the government of the Weimar Republic, existed for just eight months, and yet it became an icon of modern architecture.

Its fame is, of course, grounded in the building itself, but what also contributed to its reputation were the pictures taken of the pavilion by a photographer in collaboration with Mies van der Rohe. These photographs – a total of 16 prints from 14 glass negatives (now lost) – were all that remained after the building was demolished in February 1930. What one sees when visiting the original site nowadays is a reconstruction dating to 1986 to mark the 100-year anniversary of the architect's birth.

Mies van der Rohe had personally chosen the site for its two advantages: the backdrop provided by the Montjuïc, whose trees formed an ideal contrast to the austere, clear architecture, and because visitors to the World's Fair would have to walk through the pavilion to reach the steps behind it leading to the Spanish Village, one of the main attractions at the fair.

A few stairs lead to a platform, a terrace, which is divided into two areas: an open-air section with a large pool and a small, roofed utility room, and a single-storey, flat-roofed construction with a small pool, both of which are connected with a travertine wall.

The key features of the pavilion are the freedom with which the planes are imbued and its separate use of supports and walls. The large, flat roof is supported not by the walls but by two rows of four chrome-plated steel columns. The architect was therefore able to relieve the walls – made of the finest marble and glass – of any load–bearing function. In doing so he created spaces and planes in which roofed and open-air sections of a larger space could be positioned in relation to one another. They interpenetrate and flow into one another. One might say that Mies van der Rohe dissolved the traditional house and dissected it into its constituent parts. He did not have to pay heed to functionality as the pavilion was a piece of exhibition architecture, which left the architect free to realise his ideas and notions of the ideal without constraints – a 'pure' architecture, so to speak. Mies van der Rohe also designed the famous Barcelona Chair and Stool for the pavilion. These pieces of furniture were used by the king and queen of Spain during their visit. 'Well, I could hardly have put out simple kitchen chairs.'

Those who have carefully studied the ornately designed and organic style of Antoni Gaudí's buildings in Barcelona and then step into Mies van der Rohe's Barcelona pavilion will discover that the clarity of this model structure of modern architecture constitutes one of the greatest contrasts imaginable. Gaudí, who focused almost exclusively on the Sagrada Família (see page 150) during his final years, died after being hit by a tram in 1926. It is exciting and interesting to imagine what these two exceptional and very different architects might have said to one another on the subject of architecture if they had had the opportunity to talk.

'ARCHITECTURE IS A LANGUAGE WITH THE DISCIPLINE OF A
GRAMMAR. ONE CAN USE LANGUAGE DAY TO DAY
AS PROSE AND, IF ONE IS VERY GOOD, ONE CAN BE A POET.'

Ludwig Mies van der Rohe

LUDWIG MIES VAN DER ROHE, **THE BARCELONA PAVILION,** 1929, RECONSTRUCTION, 1986

PIERRE CHAREAU, **THE MAISON DE VERRE, PARIS,** 1928–31

73

PIERRE CHAREAU
MAISON DE VERRE, PARIS

Atenant's refusal to move out tends to cause significant problems during renovations, reconstruction or rebuilding. But it can also lead architects to find unusual and exceptional architectural solutions. This was the case at Rue Saint-Guillaume 31 in Paris. The tenant of the top floor of an 18th-century town house refused to move out, and so the new building had to be constructed beneath her feet.

The architects Pierre Chareau and Bernard Bijvoet turned this constraint into a true masterpiece, which lies hidden away in a Paris courtyard. Instead of tearing down the entire wing of the *palais*, they managed to prop up the top floor with a steel structure while the two lower floors were demolished. In its place they erected a three-storey structure that is almost as deep as the old building. Its ceilings are suspended between the supports. The front and back of the building feature floor-to-ceiling windows made almost entirely of glass blocks – hence its name: 'glass house'. This new structure was intended to house the apartment and, most importantly, the practice of Dr. Jean Dalsace. A balcony was attached to the side of the private apartment facing the garden, and each storey features transparent windows.

With its interlacing and constructive peculiarities, the Maison de Verre is a real gem. The doctor's practice is situated on the ground floor, and the private rooms such as the large living area, dining room and kitchen are on the first floor. The family's bedrooms are on the second floor. The three storeys are connected with one another at different points. The space above the waiting room on the ground floor extends into the first floor. The large living room partially extends to the first and second storeys, and the doctor's office on the side facing the garden on the ground floor extends up to the first floor. This interlacing of the various storeys results in a multitude of views and connections.

Chareau the architect was also a furniture designer and interior designer. For the Maison de Verre, he created a variety of astonishing pieces of furniture and interior-design elements reminiscent of the imagination of a number of French film directors. Throughout the building, there are cupboards that can be turned, stairs shifted, mirrors moved, tables enlarged and entire rooms hidden behind metal sliding doors.

Unfortunately, this gem of surprises is currently closed to visitors.

PIERRE CHAREAU was born in Paris in 1883. He initially became famous as a furniture designer and interior designer. In 1925 he caused a great stir with his interior design for the French embassy at the Éxposition Internationale des Arts Décoratifs et Modernes in Paris. He designed several buildings, including the Maison der Verre and the Beauvallon Golf Club (1926), with the Dutch architect Bernard Bijvoet (1889–1979). Many of his pieces of furniture were created in collaboration with the master metalsmith Louis Dalbet, and many of them are still produced today. Chareau emigrated to the USA in 1939, and he built a studio house there for Robert Motherwell in 1948. Chareau died in 1950 in East Hampton.

'THE QUALITY OF CHRYSLER COMES FROM ITS ABILITY
TO BE ROMANTIC AND IRRATIONAL AND YET NOT QUITE SO FOOLISH
AS TO BE LAUGHABLE; IT STOPS JUST SHORT, AND THEREFORE RETAINS
A SHRED OF CREDIBILITY AMIDST THE FANTASY –
RATHER LIKE NEW YORK ITSELF.'

Paul Goldberger

WILLIAM VAN ALEN, **THE CHRYSLER BUILDING, NEW YORK,** 1928–30

74

WILLIAM VAN ALEN
CHRYSLER BUILDING, NEW YORK

The architect William Van Alen made it perfectly clear that he had no truck with tradition: 'I don't want any old stuff. No perverse copying of portals, pillars and bay windows. I – I am new! Avanti!' He wanted his contribution to the Manhattan skyline to match the spirit of the times, both inside and out. And it should also break the height record of the time.

Beginning in the autumn of 1928, a 71-storey building could be seen shooting skywards in the vicinity of Grand Central Station. The circumference of the tower tapers as it rises upwards in order to comply with New York building regulations. These regulations decreed that, from the 13th floor upwards, high-rises were not allowed to occupy more than a quarter of the ground space they were built on – so as not to steal all the light from the immediate neighbourhood. As long as they corresponded to this 'wedding cake' style, there was no limit to the heights that skyscrapers were permitted to reach. The Chrysler Building incorporated all the latest technical refinements: the radiators were built into the walls; an extraction system removed dust; the cable system installed in the floors guaranteed the availability of power everywhere – the list extends to the record speed with which refuse was disposed of. The façade in particular was in line with the times. After the automobile tycoon Walter P. Chrysler took over the building project, the office tower was transformed into a glittering manifesto of the modern age. As an act of homage to the client, a large amount of metal found its way onto the façade: eagle heads, hubcaps, radiator grilles and engine hoods gleamed from the recesses of the building. Steel arches were mounted on each side of the spire: at night their triangular windows turn into spectacular peaks which vie with the illuminated building itself. The façade is covered with extravagant Art Deco designs: zigzag patterns, triangles and squares of light grey bricks and white marble. Few of these details were discernible from the narrow street grid of New York, so the entrance and the top of the tower became the real distinguishing features of the high-rise. The crown of the Chrysler Building also tells of the race to complete the world's tallest building, which was fought out in the New York of the 1920s.

Leading the way at the time was the Bank of Manhattan Trust Building at 283 metres, but what Chrysler and his master builder had in mind took everyone by surprise. The architect had a 56-metre-high spire constructed in secret inside the building, hidden from prying eyes. It took just 90 minutes to heave it onto the roof – and with an overall height of 319 metres the Chrysler Building was assured of the world record, surpassing even the Eiffel Tower. But it remained at the top for only a short while. A year later, in 1931, the Empire State Building overtook the Chrysler Building by more than 60 metres to set a new record of 381 metres.

WILLIAM VAN ALEN was born in Brooklyn in 1882. He studied there at the Pratt Institute School of Architecture. While doing so, and then after completing his studies, he worked in various New York architect's offices. He subsequently travelled to Europe, where he studied at the École des Beaux-Arts in Paris. After returning to New York, he abandoned the neo-Classical style, which had distinguished his designs until then. Van Alen became world-famous as an architect after designing the Chrysler Building in Manhattan. He died in New York in 1954.

Bold Art Deco shapes decorate the Chrysler Building on East 42nd Street in Manhattan: zigzag elements, daring points and lines ascend from the ground floor to the tip of the skyscraper. The emphasis on metal also pays homage to the man who commissioned the building, automobile tycoon Walter P. Chrysler.

WILLIAM VAN ALEN, **THE CHRYSLER BUILDING, NEW YORK,** 1928–30

75

SHREVE, LAMB AND HARMON
EMPIRE STATE BUILDING, NEW YORK

Those whose minds wander to the teachings of Sigmund Freud when considering skyscrapers and the people who build them may have a point. The Empire State Building was the response of John J. Raskob, the number two at General Motors, to the Chrysler Building (see page 190), which had been commissioned by Walter P. Chrysler, the head of the Chrysler Corporation, which, in turn, had been a reaction to the Bank of Manhattan. My building is bigger than yours!

All this against the backdrop of the economic depression – and the timing was no coincidence. At no other time would conditions have been quite so favourable. In October 1929 the New York Stock Exchange experienced a catastrophic drop before eventually collapsing altogether. Wages sank dramatically and masses of labourers became willing to work for low wages. At the height of the construction phase, 3,439 people were involved in erecting the tallest building in the world.

What was new about the Empire State Building was not its construction method. It was a conventional steel structure with ceilings of concrete and curtain walls made of brick. The innovation related to the organisation of the building site. Work on the foundations began in January 1930, and New Yorkers became witness to a unique development in construction once the steel supports were delivered to the site on 7 April of that year. The Empire State Building grew at a rate of four storeys per week. The steel supports were cast in Pittsburgh with a tolerance of just three millimetres. It took 20 hours to transport them to New Jersey by train, then by ship to Manhattan, and finally by lorry to the building site, where they were incorporated into the construction. Sometimes they were still warm from having been recently cast. As many as 500 lorries a day drove through the city along predetermined routes. That is how smoothly and perfectly the cogs turned. When the opening was celebrated on 31 May 1931, the tallest building in the world, measuring 381.6 metres, had been completed in a breathtaking 13 months. The Empire State Building was an immediate success with New Yorkers, and became a symbol of everything that New York stands for.

The Empire State Building was not a financial success, however. On the contrary: although one million dollars in entrance fees for the viewing platform were collected during the first year, the rent payments during this period no more than equalled this figure. Less than one-third of the office space had been rented by the time the building opened. The office space was not fully leased until 1950. The large number of vacancies prompted New Yorkers to nickname the skyscraper 'Empty State Building'.

Measuring 381.6 metres, the Empire State Building remained the tallest building in the world until it was surpassed in 1972 by the towers of the World Trade Center. The building's step-by-step narrowing towards the top is the result of a New York City building regulation that aimed to ensure that enough daylight and air reached the streets in the canyons between the skyscrapers.

The photographer Lewis Hine (1874–1940) documented the progress of its construction, creating what is probably the most famous series of photographs of New York. He captured the hazardous work performed by the labourers, who carried out highly complicated tasks on the steel supports without safety measures. The series can be accessed via the New York Public Library homepage.

'I HAD DISCOVERED THE CROWNING ERROR OF THE CITY, ITS
PANDORA'S BOX. FULL OF VAUNTING PRIDE THE NEW YORKER HAD CLIMBED
HERE AND SEEN WITH DISMAY WHAT HE HAD NEVER SUSPECTED, THAT
THE CITY WAS NOT THE ENDLESS SUCCESSION OF
CANYONS HE HAD SUPPOSED BUT THAT IT HAD LIMITS [...]. AND WITH
THE AWFUL REALIZATION THAT NEW YORK WAS **A CITY**
AFTER ALL AND **NOT A UNIVERSE**, THE WHOLE SHINING EDIFICE THAT
HE HAD REARED IN HIS IMAGINATION CAME **CRASHING TO THE GROUND.**'

F. Scott Fitzgerald

SHREVE, LAMB, AND HARMON, **THE EMPIRE STATE BUILDING, NEW YORK,** 1930/31

76

FRANK LLOYD WRIGHT
FALLINGWATER, PENNSYLVANIA

Architecture, Frank Lloyd Wright believed, must be created in harmonious interplay with its environment. The house the architect built near Pittsburgh achieved the complete unity of nature and architecture. At the heart of the design is a waterfall in the Bear Run River that snakes through the hilly terrain.

The Pittsburgh-based businessman Edgar J. Kaufmann planned to build a country home in the forested Allegheny Mountains. He turned to Wright, whose first suggestion during a site visit was to change the location. Instead of building the house so that it looked onto the waterfall, the architect declared, it should be built into the shelves of rock above the waterfall, and be surrounded by water. Wright later reminisced that he had built the house for people who wanted to listen to the music of the falling water.

As a reinforced concrete structure, Frank Lloyd Wright's design was on the cutting edge of the engineering fashion of its time, but it is so perfectly integrated into the natural environment that the impression is that of an archaic building growing out of the cliffs themselves. The outdoor living quarters at Fallingwater take up as much space as do the enclosed spaces. The three-storey building has no main façade; jutting balconies, terraces and staggered wall surfaces appear to blend into one another under the flat roofs. The visual appearance is shaped by both natural stone, which comes from a quarry near the house, and concrete: the balustrades of the outdoor areas are executed in reinforced concrete that has been painted ochre.

Inside, the light-filled rooms are dominated by natural materials. Stone has been layered to form slabs that jut out in some places, while in other places wood planks have been inserted as shelves. The floors throughout the house are covered in polished natural stone tiles. Low fittings for cupboards and shelves are made of walnut wood, and tables and work surfaces protrude from stone walls. The walls and floors in the bathrooms are made of cork. The window frames of steel have been painted red and contrast with the natural hues. The horizontal is emphasised on the inside as well as the outside, in keeping with the architect's tastes: he had already incorporated strip-like surfaces and overhanging roofs into his so-called Prairie Houses. Fallingwater's open room plan, which he adopted from Japanese architecture, is also characteristic of Wright.

Fallingwater was completed in 1939. The architect was already more than 70 years old by then, but had another two decades of productive work to look forward to (see page 204).

FRANK LLOYD WRIGHT was born in Richland Center, Wisconsin, in 1867. At the age of 20 he began to work in the architectural office of Louis Henry Sullivan and Dankmar Adler in Chicago. In 1893 he set up his own office and initially worked primarily on homes, which he wanted to build in unison with their inhabitants and the nature that surrounded them. His first so-called Prairie Houses were built around 1900 in the suburbs of Chicago: low buildings with flexible room plans that were in harmony with their surroundings, such as the Frederick C. Robie House. Wright also built public buildings, churches and commercial buildings. In 1943 he began to design New York's Guggenheim Museum, which was constructed between 1957 and 1959. Wright died in 1959 in Phoenix, Arizona, shortly before the museum was completed.

FRANK LLOYD WRIGHT, **FALLINGWATER, PENNSYLVANIA,** 1936–39

'I AM THE THING THAT MEN DENIED,
THE RIGHT TO BE, THE URGE TO LIVE;
AND I AM THAT WHICH MEN DEFIED, YET I ASK NAUGHT FOR WHAT I GIVE.
MY ARMS ARE FLUNG ACROSS THE DEEP,
INTO THE CLOUDS MY TOWERS SOAR, AND WHERE THE WATERS NEVER SLEEP,
I GUARD THE CALIFORNIA SHORE.'

Joseph B. Strauss

JOSEPH B. STRAUSS, **THE GOLDEN GATE BRIDGE, SAN FRANCISCO, 1933–37**

77

JOSEPH B. STRAUSS
GOLDEN GATE BRIDGE, SAN FRANCISCO

S an Francisco experienced a meteoric rise in the number of its inhabitants as a result of a gold rush in the mid-19th century. Its population increased from only 1,000 in 1848 to more than 30,000 just four years later. And by 1930 the number of people living in San Francisco had soared to more than 630,000. Many residents owned cars, which were now causing traffic problems.

San Francisco expanded at a time when most goods reached the city by ship. The new mobility and the railway, which ended in Oakland, meant that the city's geographical location was a problem in itself. Bounded to the west by the Pacific, to the east by a bay and to the north by the Golden Gate strait, there were just two ways to leave the city. Either one drove around the bay in a southerly direction, which at the time was a day's journey, or one used the ferries. When these reached the limits of their capacity in the 1920s, the city finally decided to erect a bridge for motor traffic. The idea of building a bridge had already been raised in the 1870s, but the technical obstacles were still insurmountable at that time. The Bay Bridge (1933–36) was built in the west, and a virtually impossible project was undertaken in the north: a bridge across the Golden Gate. In 1921 an engineer specialising in bridge construction, Joseph B. Strauss (1870–1938), who had already made a name for himself with other important projects, was commissioned. His first design was a piece of pure engineering, lacking any elegance. Two proven experts in the construction of suspension bridges, Leon S. Moisseiff and Othmar Ammann, who had played important parts in the building of the Manhattan and the George Washington bridges in New York, joined the project. Together they developed the plan for what was at the time the longest suspension bridge, measuring a total of 2,740 metres. Construction began on 5 January 1933, and after just four years, on 27 May 1937, more than 200,000 people walked across the bridge during the opening ceremony. The *San Francisco Chronicle* referred to it as a '35 million dollar steel harp'. The technical specifications of the Golden Gate Bridge are impressive. With a span of 1,280 metres between the pylons, it remained the longest suspension bridge in the world until the Verrazano-Narrows Bridge was built in New York in 1964. The two pylons are 227 metres high, weigh 22,000 tonnes each, and each bears a load of 61,500 tonnes. The 2,332-metre-long cables attached to the pylons are 92 centimetres thick, and each consists of 27,572 galvanised wires that had to be individually pulled across the supports before being gathered into bundles. The road surface is 19 metres wide and suspended 75 metres above the water level.

During the dangerous construction of the Golden Gate Bridge, **SAFETY** became, for the first time, an important issue. Workers had to wear protective helmets and a safety net was installed beneath the bridge, saving the lives of 19 labourers. The nets were removed after the bridge was opened, and the bridge became a favourite final destination for those who wanted to end their lives. More than 1,500 people have so far jumped over the barrier, which is just 1.2 metres high. In June 2014 the decision was made to install a steel net to deter people from jumping. Bridge manager D. Mulligan had this to say: 'It would hurt to land in a steel net seven metres down. People who are tired of life want to kill themselves, not injure themselves.'

'I SEE MY OWN HOUSE NOT SO MUCH AS A HOME (ALTHOUGH THAT IS WHAT IT IS FOR ME) BUT AS A CLEARING HOUSE OF IDEAS, WHICH CAN LATER CRYSTALLISE IN MY OWN WORK OR IN THAT OF OTHERS.'

Philip Johnson

PHILIP JOHNSON, **GLASS HOUSE, NEW CANAAN, CONNECTICUT**, 1945–49

78
PHILIP JOHNSON
GLASS HOUSE, CONNECTICUT

The architect Philip Johnson admitted that he found it difficult to work in his own house. His explanation was startling: 'There are far too many squirrels outside.' The connection becomes clear when one takes a look at the home that the American built for himself.

At first glance the building does not look much like a home. In fact it looks more like a frame for the landscape that surrounds it: a glass box set on an expansive lawn dotted with individual tall trees. It is not immediately apparent that the building has walls, because all of the 'walls' consist of glass. Nature itself has been used as a room, as the architecture critic Arthur Drexler said of the design. The natural boundaries may change with the seasons, and yet these walls are firm. Visually, they are not really perceived as boundaries; neither is the steel frame that bears the weight of the construction. The only non-transparent element is a walled brick structure with a cylindrical footprint. It houses the technical installations and the bathroom. The dark-red structure protrudes slightly above the flat roof and is the only dash of colour in the one-room house, the rest of which melts seamlessly into its surroundings.

By using steel and glass, Philip Johnson was able to develop his design to the point where it is barely seen as an enclosed space. The concept of flowing rooms without load-bearing walls had been explored a few years earlier by the architect Ludwig Mies van der Rohe – his glass Farnsworth House in Illinois probably served as a model for Johnson's own home, which marks the beginning of the latter's career as an architect. Johnson had previously made a name for himself as a theoretician: he had been the head of the architecture department at New York's Museum of Modern Art, where he curated exhibitions about contemporary architecture.

After building his own home entirely of glass in the mid-1940s, Johnson also experimented with other materials for the neighbouring buildings. He gradually expanded his property in Connecticut to include a guest house and a pavilion by the lake, and he added gallery buildings for his paintings and sculptures. In order to be able to work in a concentrated manner in the midst of nature, despite the presence of squirrels, the architect finally opted for a pragmatic solution: in 1980 he built a little stone house as a separate study on the green property – with just one small window in it.

PHILIP JOHNSON was born in Cleveland, Ohio, in 1906. After studying philology at Harvard, he established an architecture and design department at New York's Museum of Modern Art in 1930, of which he later also became the head. In 1932 Johnson published the influential exhibition catalogue *The International Style. Architecture Since 1922* together with Henry-Russell Hitchcock. Johnson was in his mid-30s when he began to study architecture, under Walter Gropius and Marcel Breuer, amongst others. In 1942 he became an independent architect. From 1954 to 1958 he and Mies van der Rohe built the Seagram Building in New York. Johnson built a large number of museum buildings, in which he also included historicising elements. In collaboration with John Burgee, the architect built the AT&T Building (today the Sony Building) in New York between 1979 and 1984. In 1979 Johnson was the first recipient of the prestigious Pritzker Prize. He died in 2005 in New Canaan, Connecticut.

79

LE CORBUSIER
NOTRE-DAME DU HAUT, RONCHAMP

The architect had not immediately been enthusiastic about his most recent commission. It took quite a lot of persuasion before Le Corbusier agreed to take on the task of developing a new design for the small church of Notre Dame du Haut: 'A pilgrimage chapel? That interests me. That is a mathematical problem with volumes and quantities!'

The celebrated architect was commissioned to build a new chapel to replace the one destroyed during the war on that very spot. It was to be entirely to his liking as he had been given carte blanche regarding its design. Le Corbusier looked forward to the task, for which he wanted to achieve harmony between the architecture and the landscape. The building's isolated position on a hill in the foothills of the Vosges provided the spatial backdrop. In terms of size, the architect had to negotiate a set of complex demands: the church in the parish of Belfort needed to accommodate a congregation of about 200 people, except when it became a place of pilgrimage twice a year. On Marian feast days, thousands of people went on a pilgrimage to the chapel above the village of Ronchamp. The design for Notre Dame du Haut would have to take this into account. Construction began in 1954, and it was consecrated the following year. Its appearance is governed by the use of concrete, which Le Corbusier admitted was his absolute favourite: 'Concrete is a material that does not cheat [...], "béton brut" says: I am concrete.' In Ronchamp the partially whitewashed concrete façade contrasts with the green, gently undulating landscape that surrounds the building. The chapel lies on the peak plateau approached by pilgrims from the south. The heavy, upward-curving roof that looks like a sail caught by a gust of wind shapes the viewer's first impression. The shape of the thick wall beneath it is warped in the south, and openings of different sizes with colourful discs are distributed at irregular intervals, making the façade appear as though it has been pierced. In the south-east corner the wall tapers into a prow-like tip and then flows back into a straight line. The east wall is concave and before it stands an outside altar, protected by a protruding roof, for masses celebrated in the open air. The north wall is dominated by right angles, and the west wall is a windowless surface that curves inwards. The main tower is located in the south-west corner. Responses to the unique chapel were sharply divided. The local papers dismissed Le Corbusier's architectural sculpture as a 'spiritual garage' and 'bedroom slipper'. But Notre Dame du Haut has long since outgrown its status as a 'concrete pile' and has become an architectural icon – perhaps even the most famous church of the 20th century.

Charles-Édouard Jeanneret, who later called himself **LE CORBUSIER**, was born in La-Chaux-de-Fonds in the French part of Switzerland in 1887. He worked in the studio of the Perret brothers in 1908/09, and was employed by Peter Behrens in Berlin the following year. In 1914 he presented his 'dom-ino' system for a two-storey building that is supported by nothing more than a reinforced concrete skeleton. He went on to create radically modern structures such as the Villa Savoy near Paris (1929–31). The Unité d'Habitation residential community in Marseille was Le Corbusier's first realised urban planning project, executed in the mid-20th century. The government buildings of the state of Punjab in its capital city, Chandigarh, were built according to his plans shortly thereafter. Le Corbusier died in 1965 in Roquebrune-Cap-Martin, on the Côte d'Azur.

'THIS IS THE MOST REVOLUTIONARY ARCHITECTURAL WORK
TO BE CREATED FOR A LONG TIME.'

Le Corbusier

LE CORBUSIER, **NOTRE-DAME DU HAUT, RONCHAMP,** 1954/55

80

FRANK LLOYD WRIGHT
SOLOMON R. GUGGENHEIM MUSEUM, NEW YORK

Frank Lloyd Wright's new building to house the Guggenheim Museum in the middle of Manhattan had divided the art world into two camps since the first drafts were made public. Committed supporters had to defend their opinions against critics, to whom the new Guggenheim was anything but a museum. The architect's own verdict on his revolutionary architectural sculpture was emphatic: 'I don't give a damn what it's used for; I wanted to build a building like this one.'

New York's Guggenheim Museum ushered in a new era for the architectural demands made on museums: to begin with, architecture now drew attention to itself before it even considered the art in its interior. The collection of abstract painting amassed by the industrialist Solomon R. Guggenheim set the tone for the new building. The curator Hilla Rebay contacted the architect Frank Lloyd Wright in 1943: 'I want a temple of the spirit, a monument,' she said of her plans. Over the course of the next decade and a half, Wright presented countless designs for a museum in Manhattan, and in 1956 the building finally began to take shape: an ivory-coloured sculpture jutting out of the row of buildings lining New York's Fifth Avenue. It consists of a substructure upon which rest several round discs whose diameter increases progressively. The building constituted an architectural novelty that transcended all traditions, so that it was not long before the first criticisms were voiced. The building was said by one critic to resemble an overturned cupcake, while another claimed it was reminiscent of a washing machine. The collector and niece of the founder, Peggy Guggenheim, noted that the museum looked like an enormous garage, and she was particularly critical of the building's cramped position and the lack of focus on the art that it housed, a thought echoed by the majority of early visitors.

The building's suitability for the presentation of works of art is, after all, limited. Inside the building a long ramp winds its way along the wall from the ground floor to the top floor. The large central area surrounded by this spiral is illuminated by a skylight. Wright had detailed plans for the route to be taken by visitors: they would first take the lift up to the top, and then wander along step by step to explore the art. But how should art be presented on crooked walls? Even the artists themselves feared that their works of art, for which the museum had after all been constructed, would be at a disadvantage. The architect Philip Johnson drastically described the building as architecture that defies all art. Wright was not swayed, and continued to build his 'uninterrupted, beautiful symphony'. The architect did not live to see the opening of the museum, for he died just a few months before it was completed in 1959. Nor was he able to witness the Guggenheim's rapid rise to fame. It was not long before the museum became one of New York's landmarks.

FRANK LLOYD WRIGHT, **THE SOLOMON R. GUGGENHEIM MUSEUM, NEW YORK,** 1957–59

The spiral on Fifth Avenue in New York has curled upwards since it was built by Wright in 1959. Many critics feared that the art in the rotunda would become a sideshow. There was even talk of a war between painting and architecture, 'from which both will emerge wounded'.

'LESS IS MORE.'

Ludwig Mies van der Rohe

LUDWIG MIES VAN DER ROHE, **THE SEAGRAM BUILDING, NEW YORK,** 1958

81

LUDWIG MIES VAN DER ROHE
SEAGRAM BUILDING, NEW YORK

Alcohol no doubt has its positive sides. One of them is when it generates so much income for a company and its owner that they can afford to dispense with 60 per cent of a buildable piece of land when constructing the company headquarters on Park Avenue in New York – one of the most expensive streets in 1950s New York – simply to enable the architect to realise his vision of the ideal skyscraper.

The business in question was the Canadian liquor conglomerate Seagram Company Ltd., the owner was Samuel Bronfman and the architect was Ludwig Mies van der Rohe. The stage was set in 1954, but there was just one problem: a New York building regulation from 1916 stipulating that all buildings above a certain height had to be built with setbacks – steplike recessions in the profile of tall buildings – to ensure that enough sunlight and air reached the streets between skyscrapers. Mies, however, wanted to build a skyscraper without recessions, a stepless block. So he made what must have seemed an impossible suggestion: that the skyscraper be built away from the street canyon, using only 40 per cent of the available building site. The unused land was to be made into a publicly accessible plaza in front of the skyscraper. When a property becomes available on Park Avenue, the general idea is to use every square metre of building land – resulting in a row of skyscrapers and high-rise buildings whose façades reach all the way to the pavement. Fortunately, Bronfman and his daughter Phyllis Lambert, who had recommended Mies for the commission, agreed to the suggestion, clearing the way for the construction of what is, architectonically speaking, probably the most important skyscraper of the 20th century. This, too, confirmed Mies's dictum that 'Less is more': that architecture becomes special not only through what is built, but also through what is not built.

Mies van der Rohe's Seagram Building, completed in 1958, was and continues to be an exceptional piece of architecture in every respect. It is rare for a high-rise office building – this was Mies's first – to feature such an unostentatious, clear and elegant design. It is a steel-frame construction with a curtain wall like that already used by Gropius in 1911 for the Fagus factory (see page 172) – the difference being that the Seagram Building is 39 storeys high, and not just three. As Mies had declared as early as 1922, laying bare the invisible construction elements was a priority for him. Here, they are made visible by the double-T sections, which were specially cast in bronze.

Mies was an admirer of classical Greece. Through its simplicity and perfection, combined with the precious materials, his building takes on the character of a sculpture transferred to the modern age. The plaza gives it the grand appearance it deserves.

LUDWIG MIES VAN DER ROHE
was born in Aachen in 1886. He moved to Berlin in 1905 and worked for Bruno Paul and Peter Behrens until 1912. He built his first house in 1907. In 1921/22 he created his designs for a visionary skyscraper made entirely of steel and glass; it was never built, however. Mies helped to plan and oversaw the construction of the Weissenhofsiedlung housing estate in Stuttgart in 1927, designed the Barcelona Pavilion in 1929 and realised the Villa Tugendhat in Brno from 1928 to 1930. That same year, he became director of the Bauhaus in Dessau, which was closed down by the Nazis in 1933. In 1937 Mies emigrated to the USA, became a professor in Chicago, and established his own office in 1939. Buildings for the Illinois Institute of Technology and apartment buildings in Chicago followed. His last great project was the Neue Nationalgalerie in Berlin in 1967. Mies died in 1969 in Chicago.

82

OSCAR NIEMEYER
NATIONAL CONGRESS AND CATHEDRAL, BRASÍLIA

Oscar Niemeyer wanted to make visitors to the new capital of Brazil 'feel surprised and moved'. His buildings in the planned city of Brasília were to be entirely different from everything that had ever existed. The architect was determined to escape from the architectural routine of his time.

Brasília was the perfect place for this. President Juscelino Kubitschek de Oliveira was the one who initiated the project, but gave his planners entirely free rein. Oscar Niemeyer was in charge of the design of the prestigious buildings, and Lúcio Costa was commissioned with the urban planning. Kubitschek set no parameters for the city's layout or its architecture except one: the new capital city, situated in the geographical centre of the country, was to be completed in the space of three years.

And so, starting in 1957, a modern planned city was constructed in the middle of nowhere, far away from other big cities. It was built from the ground up by 80,000 labourers in record time. Costa designed a cross with two axes. The first was built for residential areas and the second was conceived as the Monumental Axis, lined by public buildings. It culminates in Three Powers Plaza, consisting of the Supreme Court, the National Congress and the Presidential Office. Niemeyer developed a unique formal vocabulary for Brasília. The National Congress is a flat-roofed building overshadowed by a pair of high-rise buildings containing the offices of the deputies. On the roof of the National Congress are two concrete structures: a dome on the left above the Senate, and a bowl on the right above the Chamber of Deputies. A ramp and four bridges lead up to the white-marble-clad roof, which is accessible to pedestrians.

The cathedral is located a little way away from the square, but also on the Monumental Axis. Niemayer stated that this was, without a doubt, 'one of the most attractive subjects for any architect. Thanks to the simplicity of the model, where the sacred act is concerned, it permits the greatest liberty of conception.' Niemeyer took advantage of this liberty to design a circular shape. And what a shape it is! Sickle-shaped ribs of concrete converge in a bundle, with panes of frosted glass between them. His choice of material – concrete reinforced with steel – is one reason the architect was so free to choose his design language for Brasília. 'We experimented to find out what could be done with reinforced concrete,' Niemeyer later said. 'Reinforced concrete opened up possibilities for my generation that had not existed until then.'

OSCAR NIEMEYER was born in Rio de Janeiro in 1907. After studying there at the Escola Nacional de Belas Artes, he designed public buildings and private houses in Brazil and worked as a city planner. Niemeyer got to know the architect Le Corbusier, and together they designed the United Nations building in New York in 1947. Niemeyer's construction material of choice was concrete, which he formed into increasingly sculptural shapes. From 1956 to 1961 he was the chief architect of Brazil's new capital city: Brasília. Niemeyer left the country during the military dictatorship and resettled in France. In Europe, too, he realised numerous buildings, including the main office of the Mondadori publishing company in Milan. In 1988 he was awarded the Pritzker Prize. Oscar Niemeyer died in Rio de Janeiro in 2012, at the age of 104.

'WE WATCHED THE CITY
GROW LIKE A FLOWER
IN THE WILDERNESS.'

Oscar Niemeyer

OSCAR NIEMEYER, **NATIONAL CONGRESS, BRASÍLIA**, 1958–60

'THE SUN NEVER KNEW HOW GREAT
IT WAS UNTIL IT FELL ON THE SIDE
OF A BUILDING.'

Louis I. Kahn

LOUIS I. KAHN, **THE SALK INSTITUTE FOR BIOLOGICAL STUDIES, CALIFORNIA**, 1959–65

83

LOUIS I. KAHN
SALK INSTITUTE FOR BIOLOGICAL STUDIES, CALIFORNIA

The term 'Brutalism', as used to describe an architectural style of the 1950s and 1960s, is slightly misleading. Although such buildings and their raw, grey walls can at first glance evoke associations with violence and brutality, this has nothing at all to do with it. The term originates from the French *béton brut*, which means 'raw or exposed concrete'.

Exposed concrete is unplastered concrete, the way it looks after the shuttering boards have been removed. The Swedish architect Hans Asplund coined the term in 1950. The first building to fall under this category is the school built by architects Alison and Peter Smithson in the English town of Hunstanton between 1949 and 1954 – although it is worth noting that Le Corbusier had already used exposed concrete for his Unité d'Habitation in Marseille (1945–52).

Louis I. Kahn is one of the most important protagonists of this style, and the Salk Institute for Biological Studies, built in La Jolla, California, between 1959 and 1965, is one of his most famous buildings. The research institution was founded by the physician and immunologist Jonas Salk, who developed the polio vaccine. He wanted to create a research centre that would employ the best scientists. Alongside professional considerations, the attractive location and impressive architecture were important, or even critical, in winning them over: architecture as seduction.

The aim was to create a campus-like atmosphere. To this end Kahn designed a central courtyard with two wings housing offices and laboratories. Each of the functional rooms is accompanied by a small area for retreating and thinking, for discussing or just contemplating and relaxing. All of these rooms have views of the Pacific Ocean.

The campus itself aims to facilitate outdoor meetings and exchanges between the scientists. The conscious direction of light and shade and the austere symmetry could be described as Kahn's trademarks, like the use of exposed concrete. A small waterway is set into the central axis of the courtyard, imbuing the ascetic-looking building with an almost monastic atmosphere. The two predominant building materials are mahogany, which was used for window frames and screens, and exposed concrete.

Kahn's buildings are always grand in some way, while also having a martial – even monumental – air that is the result of the austerity and majesty of the elemental forms. In that sense, the term 'Brutalism' seems appropriate. And yet, when it comes to concrete, it all depends on what you do with it.

Born in Estonia in 1901, **LOUIS ISADORE KAHN** emigrated to the USA with his family in 1906. He studied architecture at the University of Philadelphia. He opened his own office in 1934 and became a professor of architecture at Yale University in 1947. He first set foot on the international stage when he built the Yale University Art Gallery in New Haven (1952–54). After the Salk Institute, in La Jolla, California (1959–65), he created the impressive Indian Institute of Management in Ahmedabad, India, between 1962 and 1974, and worked on the construction of the Sangsad Bhaban, or National Parliament House, in Dhaka, the capital of Bangladesh, from 1963 until his death. Kahn died of a heart attack in 1974 at a train station in New York. As he was not carrying sufficient identification, it took days before Kahn's family found out that he had died.

'ONE PERSON OPPOSITE ANOTHER, ARRANGED
IN CIRCLES IN SWEEPING, SUSPENDED ARCS AROUND
SOARING CRYSTAL PYRAMIDS.'

Hans Scharoun

HANS SCHAROUN, **THE BERLIN PHILHARMONIE,** 1957 (PLANNING), 1960–63

84

HANS SCHAROUN
PHILHARMONIE, BERLIN

Pure concert halls constructed specifically for musical performances were created in the 17th and 18th centuries, when music slowly emancipated itself from its ties to ruling houses and churches. Professional orchestras and concert associations were formed, and they needed suitable performance halls.

In contrast to theatre and opera buildings, concert halls do not need a fly tower, and so the rectangular, box-shaped building became the classic shape for concert buildings. The front houses the podium, beyond which the audience is accommodated in a long, rectangular space that can feature balconies at the sides and along the back wall. The concert building of the Wiener Musikverein (Viennese Music Association), constructed in 1868, became the measure for this type of building.

In order to optimise the acoustics, concert halls with slanted roofs and ascending seats for the audience began to emerge. The concert hall itself is developed separately from the concert building. It is like an egg in a box, an interior space perfectly suited to music. The Royal Festival Hall, constructed in London in 1951, is an example of this. When a new concert hall was to be built for the Berlin Philharmonic orchestra (established in 1882) after the destruction of the Second World War, Hans Scharoun's revolutionary concept won the competition in 1957. He positioned the orchestra in the middle of the hall and seated the audience around it. The ground plan is based on three superimposed, rotated pentagons, to which Scharoun assigned the meanings 'space', 'music' and 'humankind'. The three pentagons have formed the logo of the Berlin Philharmonic ever since.

Tiered seats rise asymmetrically from the centre, providing views of the orchestra from every side. Scharoun's description sounds more poetic. He speaks of the 'valley at the bottom of which the orchestra is to be found, surrounded by rising vineyards.'

The orchestra's podium is slightly off-centre, with the conductor's rostrum constituting the actual centre. Scharoun's concept largely dissolves not only the classic division between musicians and listeners, but also the structure of the audience: the audience is accommodated not in a block of 2,250 seats, but in a number of smaller, more intimate blocks of up to 100 seats.

There is a historical reason why the tent-like concert hall, constructed between 1960 and 1963, appears to be the wrong way round, with its back facing Potsdamer Platz. During the planning period this was the site of the boundary separating Berlin's east and west sectors, which became insurmountable with the construction of the Berlin Wall in 1961.

Young architects are often the ones who create revolutionary buildings. The Berlin Philharmonie, however, was the work of **HANS SCHAROUN** (born 1893 in Bremen), who was more than 60 years old at the time. Although he had already been a member of the avant-garde during the Expressionist period, he faded somewhat into obscurity after the triumph of Functionalism. He did not receive large commissions again until after the Second World War, and revived his avant-garde credentials when he built the Philharmonie. He was the president of the Akademie der Künste in Berlin from 1956 to 1968 and created additional masterpieces in the form of the German Embassy in Brasília from 1963 to 1971 and the Staatsbibliothek library in Berlin from 1964 onwards. Scharoun died in 1972 in Berlin.

'HUMAN LIFE IS A COMBINATION OF TRAGEDY AND COMEDY. THE FORMS AND PATTERNS THAT SURROUND US ARE THE MUSIC THAT ACCOMPANIES THIS TRAGEDY AND THIS COMEDY.'

Alvar Aalto

ALVAR AALTO, **FINLANDIA HALL, HELSINKI,** 1967–71

85

ALVAR AALTO
FINLANDIA HALL, HELSINKI

During the first two decades of the 20th century the latest developments in architecture had relatively little impact in Finland. This was quite natural, given Finland's peripheral position at the edge of Europe, but it was also the result of the rural structures in the very sparsely populated parts of the country. The aesthetic of the towns and cities was largely dominated by Nordic Neo-Classicism.

This state of affairs did not change until the arrival of architects such as Gunnar Asplund and Alvar Aalto, who incorporated international Functionalism into their own work and into Scandinavian architecture in general. Aalto's travels through the rest of Europe had a lasting effect on him, though he combined functionalist ideas with the traditions of Finnish architecture, in which wood plays a key role in construction.

Aalto's first great building to garner international acclaim was the sanatorium in Paimio, which he worked on between 1929 and 1933. His oeuvre is often described using the term 'organic architecture', which can be slightly misleading. It has nothing to do with organs, but instead refers, among other things, to the belief that form should develop out of necessity or, more succinctly, that 'form follows function'. Aalto's sanatorium for people suffering from tuberculosis functions according to this principle. The building reaches into the landscape in a fanlike form and takes into account the specific needs of the patients. Their rooms are all located in the south-facing section to ensure that they are flooded with as much light, air and warmth as possible. The communal areas are in the centre, while the functional areas, such as the kitchens and laundry rooms, are in the north.

The 1930s saw the construction of buildings in which curved shapes assume an important role. This may be a case of the architect's name influencing his work, as 'aalto' is the Finnish word for 'wave'. According to Aalto, 'An architectural solution should always have a human aim.' He felt it was important for people to feel comfortable, and he often used wood – which is omnipresent in Finland and creates a homely atmosphere – as the construction material for his buildings. He generally designed matching furniture and various other details together with his wife, with whom he founded the furniture company Artek for this purpose in 1935. Aalto's chairs and vases have become design classics.

After the Second World War, Aalto concentrated on urban-planning issues, such as the redesign of Helsinki from 1960 onwards. The construction of Finlandia Hall, which began in 1962, was part of this large-scale project. The concert and congress hall is located on Töölö Bay and is characterised by features typical of the late phase of Aalto's oeuvre, including the tower with the slanted roof. The focal point is not the form but the audience and the artists, around which the building has been designed.

ALVAR AALTO, born in Kuortane, Finland, in 1898, was perhaps the most important architect and designer in Scandinavia. He married Aino Marsio, an architect and designer, in 1924. It was his belief that the aim of architecture and design was to provide people with a better living space, and thus with a better quality of life. In 1939 he designed the Finnish Pavilion for the World's Fair in New York, which prompted Frank Lloyd Wright to declare that Aalto's was a work of genius. From 1940 he was professor of architecture at the Massachusetts Institute of Technology in Cambridge, Massachusetts. Most of his buildings are to be found in Finland. Among those he built in Germany was the Wolfsburg Cultural Centre (1958–62), which now bears his name: Alvar-Aalto-Kulturhaus. Aalto died in 1976 in Helsinki.

86

GÜNTER BEHNISCH
OLYMPIC STADIUM, MUNICH

The Olympic Games that took place in Munich in 1972 were intended to present the new Federal Republic's democratic, open side to the world. The games would be a celebration of sport for all – as well as a summer Olympiad surrounded by nature. The commissioning body wanted to steer clear of any big, unwieldy buildings and to design a park landscape instead.

This main aim was to contrast dramatically with the Olympic Games staged in Berlin in 1936. Any impression of intimidating monumentality and demonstrations of power were to be avoided at all costs. The architect Günter Behnisch, who won the competition for the design of the Olympic grounds in 1967, successfully achieved this aim. The area chosen for the games – on the north edge of the centre of Munich – had been used after the Second World War as a dumping ground for war rubble, which was later landscaped into artificial hills. Behnisch transformed the three square kilometres into a park landscape with lakes, but no clear axes and, most importantly, he put part of the complex underground. In fact only one-third of the Olympic Stadium is erected above ground level. The rest of the structures – including the enormous stands and the supply areas – were integrated into the slopes or are hidden beneath a blanket of green. The large arenas are strewn across the grounds, and are held together by a light and airy-looking roof construction: A web of translucent plates of acrylic glass and steel cables spans a surface area of almost 75,000 square metres, covering the landscape and buildings, part of the stadium and the Olympic Hall and Swimming Hall. Only 12 large pylons measuring up to 81 metres in height and 36 smaller, round supports hold up the roof. Concrete blocks hidden underground constitute the main supports. This avant-garde, web-like construction capable of covering large surface areas was developed in the 1950s. The engineer Frei Otto expanded the membrane structure to span ever-larger areas. His design for Munich's Olympic grounds was controversial among specialists as the roof was larger than all previously executed cable-net structures. His plan proved successful, however, albeit at considerable cost: the tent-like roof landscape exceeded the original estimates several times over. Behnisch and the federal, state and local authority's Olympic construction company (OBG) exchanged verbal volleys: 'I planned a Volkswagen and the OBG has turned it into a Cadillac,' claimed the architect. 'Behnisch planned a Cadillac and thought he could run it with a Volkswagen engine,' came the riposte. Whether it is a Cadillac or a VW, this much is certain: Munich's Olympic Park continues to be a popular tourist attraction and destination for outings – not to mention a milestone of high-tech architecture.

GÜNTER BEHNISCH was born in Lockwitz, near Dresden, in 1922. After his time as a prisoner of war in England, Behnisch studied architecture at the Technische Hochschule Stuttgart. One of his first commissions was for the Staatliche Fachhochschule für Technik (today the Hochschule Ulm). Construction on the grounds for the Summer Olympics in Munich began in 1968. His structures, which fulfilled a variety of functions, were known for their openness and transparency. Behnisch created kindergartens, schools and museums, the Plenary Complex of the German Parliament in Bonn and the Academy of Arts in Berlin. He also took on the redesign of Stuttgart's Schlossplatz. Behnisch died in Stuttgart in 2010.

GÜNTER BEHNISCH, **THE OLYMPIC PARK, MUNICH,** 1968–72

For the Olympic Games in Munich, Behnisch designed a park landscape of hills and lakes into which the various sports grounds were integrated. The avant-garde, tent-like roof construction caused a sensation.

87

JØRN UTZON
OPERA HOUSE, SYDNEY

The jury could be sure that its decision would have a polarising effect. But the competition for the new building had been decided: the Danish architect Jørn Utzon was to build an opera house for Sydney. As the jury stated: 'Because of its very originality, it is clearly a controversial design. We are, however, absolutely convinced of its merits.'

A small tongue of land in the city's port known as Bennelong Point was designated as the site for the new house of culture. The architect placed the opera house on a 15-metre-high plateau to which a wide staircase ascends. He positioned the 'protagonists', the larger opera hall and a smaller concert hall, in a simple substructure. The two auditoriums are not visible from outside. The eye is drawn to the shell-like roof structures, which, in the form of enormous seashells or sails, make reference to the surrounding landscape. The opera house is, after all, surrounded by water on three sides. The curved surfaces are covered in white glazed ceramic tiles that contrast with the blue of the water and reflect the sunlight.

Utzon's roof sculpture split the nation into two camps even before construction had begun. Euphoric proponents spoke of a 'piece of poetry', whereas critics saw it only as a 'Danish pastry'. The foundation stone for the new building was laid in 1959. The technical execution of the plans presented a challenge, however. The studio of the engineer Ove Arup was responsible for the structural engineering, and thus also for the innovative roof shapes. The development of the shell structures alone took 375,000 working hours. As the construction costs soared, the completion date receded, and criticism of Utzon became increasingly strident.

The architect also lost political backing for his construction project after a change of government. After a long struggle, he eventually abandoned his project and left Australia in 1966. A wave of indignation swept through the international architectural scene, which expressed solidarity with Utzon. The Australian government promptly appointed successors to complete the project. In 1973 the opera house was, at last, opened – without Utzon. It was not until the Summer Olympics in Sydney in the year 2000 that the Australian government contacted the architect to ask him to commit his design principles for the opera house to paper. And so, more than 30 years after his departure, Utzon continued to work on his masterpiece, which had long since become the city's most famous landmark.

JØRN UTZON was born in Copenhagen in 1918. After studying architecture at the local art academy, he briefly worked as an assistant in the office of Alvar Aalto in Helsinki. Utzon travelled around Europe, to Morocco and Mexico, and to the USA, in part to visit Frank Lloyd Wright and Ludwig Mies van der Rohe. In 1950 he became an independent architect. He gained international acclaim with his award-winning design for the Sydney Opera House. After the failure of the project, Utzon withdrew from the public eye, but he carried out several more large projects, including the parliament building in Kuwait, which he created together with his son Jan. In 2003 he was awarded the Pritzker Prize. Utzon died in 2008 near Copenhagen.

'THAT IS NOT AN OPERA HOUSE,
IT IS A SHELL.'

Frank Lloyd Wright

JØRN UTZON, **THE SYDNEY OPERA HOUSE,** 1959–73

'WE WILL BUILD A HALL,
    AN ENORMOUS HALL,
AND THEN WE'LL TAKE IT FROM THERE.'

Renzo Piano

RENZO PIANO AND RICHARD ROGERS, **THE CENTRE GEORGES POMPIDOU, PARIS,** 1970–77

88

RENZO PIANO UND RICHARD ROGERS
CENTRE GEORGES POMPIDOU, PARIS

The French – or at least those among them who are interested in art – are a happy people. That is to say, they were so when Georges Pompidou became president of the Grande Nation. This was because one of his first decisions was that Paris should have a modern and unique cultural centre. The commission was put out to tender in 1970. And, for the first time, foreign architects were allowed to participate.

A total of 681 proposals were submitted and the jury, which included Philip Johnson, Oscar Niemeyer and Jean Prouvé, selected Design 439. This, as it happened, had been submitted by two foreigners: the Brit Richard Rogers and the Italian Renzo Piano.

The challenge was to create a space for a museum of modern art, a library, a centre for design and an institute for contemporary music. How does one create space in a building for four completely different cultural institutions with entirely different (spatial) needs? One builds a 'factory' whose sole product is space. Vast amounts of space. As the two young architects Rogers and Piano had begun their careers with the construction of halls, their plan was to build a hall here too – the difference being that it would be enormous, albeit not be quite as huge as the gigantic plot in Beaubourg at the heart of Paris would have permitted. Just as Ludwig Mies van der Rohe had done with the Seagram Building in New York (see page 208), Rogers and Piano also left half of the available building ground as an unbuilt urban space. And as is the case with Mies's design, the space here is not merely space. It is instead an unbuilt yet incredibly important part of the architectural structure.

What Piano and Rogers had in mind was a highly unusual construction. As in a gigantic modular assembly system, they built a steel framework of trussed girders visible from every side, and mounted all access routes and functions of the building on the outside of this skeleton in order to create what they needed on the inside: space. With its steel pipes and ducts, the building does indeed look like a factory because the services pipes that are normally hidden on the inside are visible here on the outside and colour-coded. For example: blue pipes are air-conditioning ducts, green pipes are used for the water supply, yellow ones for electricity, and red is reserved for elevators and fire extinguishers. As a result, each of the six storeys has a support-free surface area of more than 7,000 square metres, which can be subdivided according to the needs of the individual departments.

The open construction with glass walls could not, unfortunately, be applied to every department. For conservation reasons the art collection has been housed in a museum within the Centre Pompidou since 1985. To accommodate the Institute of Contemporary Music's need for soundproof rooms, its rooms were moved underground and are now housed in the annexe and beneath the nearby fountain created by Jean Tinguely and Niki de Saint Phalle.

The outdoor area at ground level, reminiscent of an Italian piazza, blends into the interior, which was originally planned as an open space but was enclosed because of weather conditions. The galleries on the façade facing the square are open to the public and in this way could be said to expand the piazza in front of the building into the third dimension.

President Georges Pompidou wanted a unique, modern cultural centre. And that is what he got.

89

JAMES STIRLING
NEUE STAATSGALERIE, STUTTGART

In the 20th century, as in the preceding centuries, architectural styles succeeded one another in a series of actions and reactions. The difference was that in the 20th century the styles were more varied, partly as a result of new technical developments, and that the exchanges and changes took place more rapidly than they had in previous centuries.

The strict functionalism of buildings by architects such as Martin Gropius, the apparent coldness of designs by the likes of Le Corbusier and the monumental 'nakedness' of the Brutalism of Louis I. Kahn virtually cried out for a reaction, a stylistic countermovement that blazed the way for what became known as Post-Modernism. This was an attempt to achieve harmony between modern architecture and the historical circumstances of cities. Perhaps it was also an attempt to come up with a tongue-in-cheek reaction to the dogmatic severity of predecessors, with an 'anything goes' attitude instead of doctrine. The Neue Staatsgalerie, which Scot James Stirling began to design in 1974, sets the tone for this development, encompassing everything that constitutes Post-Modernism, a term that is generally difficult to define.

The then director of the state art collections obviously wanted defined spatial structures, perhaps as a direct response to the recently completed Centre Pompidou (see page 224). A 'container-architecture structure that applies the principle of total functionality to the entire museum complex without careful consideration' was to be avoided. Stirling therefore built an almost classical building between 1977 and 1984, with firm structures that are clearly visible on the outside. The bright pink and blue handrails provide colourful contrasts and the undulating glass walls by the entrance look like curved green waves. These are accompanied by sturdy stone-slab cladding, which further emphasises the robustness. The interior consists of a predetermined sequence of rooms that bring to mind a Baroque enfilade.

A further highlight is the cour d'honneur with a rotunda reminiscent of the Altes Museum in Berlin (see page 142), a classic piece of museum architecture. The rotunda features several references to the history of architecture, including a pair of columns, Gothic pointed arches, classical arcades, as well as other quotations ranging from Egypt to De Stijl and Bauhaus. In brief: an architectural collage.

With the Neue Staatsgalerie, Stirling simultaneously incorporates an examination of his own genre, architecture – though he clearly does so with a twinkle in his eye.

JAMES STIRLING, who was born in Glasgow in 1926, was one of the most important architects of Great Britain. He studied in Liverpool (1945–50) and opened his own office in 1956 with James Gowan. He designed a large number of buildings for British universities in the 1960s. From the point of view of style, he started out as a functionalist, though his style changed, so that he became a protagonist of Post-Modernism. The Clore Gallery of Tate Britain in London was built starting in 1980, and in 1984 Stirling designed the Arthur M. Sackler Museum at Harvard University. This consolidated his reputation as an international superstar of architecture. Stirling received countless awards, including a knighthood in 1992, the year in which he died.

JAMES STIRLING, **THE NEUE STAATSGALERIE, STUTTGART,** 1977–84

90

IEOH MING PEI
PYRAMID, MUSÉE DU LOUVRE, PARIS

It is a well-known fact that most of an iceberg's mass remains out of sight. This is not so in the case of pyramids, however. The pyramid in the Cour Napoléon at the Louvre in Paris can be seen in all its glory, but in fact it is merely the visible part of an enormous subterranean complex: the tip of an iceberg. It drew harsh criticism even before its opening, but today it is a symbol of Paris.

The Louvre (see page 110) had been the residence of France's rulers since the 13th century. Rebuilt in the Renaissance style in the 16th century, it became the main seat of French kings. When the court moved to Versailles under Louis XIV, the building was transferred to the city of Paris and it became the seat of the Académie Française. Artists' studios, cabarets and small shops also moved in. The Louvre became France's first public museum after the French Revolution, until it became Napoleon's main residence. In 1873 the President of the Republic eventually moved into the Élysée Palace and the Louvre was permanently converted into a museum: one that would eventually attract the largest number of visitors in the world, no less. This success was double-edged, however, as the building was not equipped to cope with the floods of visitors. François Mitterrand, the president of France, decided in 1981 that extensive remodelling and extensions were needed, including the north wing, which until then had been used as the French Ministry of Finance. The Grand Louvre project began.

President Mitterrand commissioned the Chinese-American architect Ieoh Ming Pei, who built underground structures beneath most of the cour d'honneur (the Louvre's inner courtyard). This provided new means by which the throngs of visitors could be channelled. The first part of the project was completed in 1989 and the critics who had initially feared that the Louvre would be entirely covered by a pyramid were assuaged by the transparent, 21-metre-high structure. In building the pyramid and the nine-metre-deep subterranean level, Pei, who believes that a museum should have a suitable entrance, created a volume and a space that is in every way appropriate. The pyramid is therefore nothing other than a discreet reference to what is happening underground. In the course of the second phase, executed in 1993, the subterranean system was further expanded and Pei built an inverted pyramid into the basement as a 'folly'.

The pyramid shape was not chosen at random, of course. Pei uses it as a reference to the Louvre's collections of antiquities and in this way joins them to the modern period. It is, furthermore, an anchor point in the cityscape that constitutes the beginning of the axis that extends to the Tuileries, the Champs-Elysées, the Arc de Triomphe and La Défense.

Born in Shanghai in 1917, **IEOH MING PEI** arrived in the USA in 1935 and studied architecture at MIT in Boston. Le Corbusier was his great role model. After the Second World War, Pei studied at the Harvard Graduate School of Design, which was under the directorship of Walter Gropius. In 1955 he opened his own office. The construction of the National Center for Atmospheric Research near Boulder, Colorado, in 1961 was his first great success. He created the annexe for the National Gallery of Art in Washington, DC, in 1968–78. In 1983 Pei was awarded the renowned Pritzker Prize and, in 1989, the Praemium Imperiale. His success with the Louvre was followed by the exhibition space for the Deutsches Historisches Museum in Berlin (1998–2003).

'THE FIRST TIME THAT I CAME TO THE LOUVRE,
IN 1951, THERE WERE JUST TWO LAVATORIES
IN THIS ENORMOUS MUSEUM, AND
NOBODY COULD FIND THEM.'

Ieoh Ming Pei

IEOH MING PEI, **THE LOUVRE PYRAMID, PARIS,** 1982–89

'THE BUILDING HAS EXCEPTIONAL, INTERESTING, GENEROUS AND FUTURISTIC SIDES. BUT IT ALSO HAS CLAUSTROPHOBIC, DIFFICULT AND DARK SIDES. THIS MIXTURE IS PART OF WHAT ONE EXPERIENCES IN THIS MUSEUM.'

Daniel Libeskind

DANIEL LIBESKIND, **THE JEWISH MUSEUM, BERLIN,** 1989–98

91

DANIEL LIBESKIND
JEWISH MUSEUM, BERLIN

The American architect Daniel Libeskind realised his first great plan in the Kreuzberg district in Berlin. In 1989 he won the competition for the expansion of the Jewish Museum when his spectacular architectural concept was chosen from among 165 submissions. The Baroque building on Lindenstrasse was to be supplemented by an annexe – and thanks to Libeskind, it would become a visitor attraction.

The historic section of the complex of buildings is a three-winged Baroque structure constructed by Johann Philipp Gerlach around 1730. It accommodates the research and documentary centre for Jewish history. The museum's permanent collection, on the other hand, is housed in the Libeskind building. The two elements are separate when viewed from the outside, and connected only by a subterranean slate staircase. The annexe's footprint is in the shape of an asymmetrical zigzag. Slit-shaped lines of windows are incised into its shiny silvery skin of zinc plate. Impenetrable series of rooms on asymmetrical storeys, dark niches and blind spots shape this part of the museum. A straight line runs through the meandering architectural layout: 'The official name of the project is "Jewish Museum" but I have named it "Between the Lines" because for me, it is about two lines of thinking, organization and relationship. One is a straight line, but broken into many fragments, the other is a tortuous line, but continuing indefinitely,' the architect has said. Five empty rooms with exposed concrete walls constitute the intersections between these two lines. According to the architect, 'the non-visible' manifests itself 'as emptiness, as the invisible' in these 'voids'. All but one of these rooms are inaccessible. They symbolise the emptiness that remains after the Holocaust. Visitors walk along three axes on floors that are not always level to reach the various focal points of the exhibition. The first and longest of the three is the 'Axis of Continuity': it connects the old building with a steep flight of stairs that rises towards the permanent exhibition. The 'Axis of Emigration' follows a continually narrowing passageway that is enclosed by slanted walls and leads to an outdoor area. Here, olive trees grow out of 49 tall concrete steles filled with soil in a rectangular garden of steles. The third axis takes the visitor to a steel door. This axis ends in front of the 24-metre-high 'Holocaust Tower', a cold, dark and entirely empty memorial space in remembrance of the victims of the Holocaust.

DANIEL LIBESKIND was born in 1946 in the Polish city of Łódź and emigrated to the USA at the age of 14. He studied music and architecture, and in 1989 he won the competition for the design of the Jewish Museum in Berlin, a project that won him the Deutscher Architekturpreis ten years later. In 2003 Libeskind's entry was selected for the design of the Freedom Tower on the grounds of the destroyed World Trade Center in New York. In addition to his work as an architect, Libeskind teaches at numerous universities worldwide. His projects include museums, business and leisure centres, as well as landscape and urban planning.

above Slanted beams jut upwards over the steep main staircase in the Jewish Museum. Light enters the staircase through narrow slits in the wall and a strip of window.

right The ground plan is based on two lines. The architect left the places in which they intersect empty. Menashe Kadishman's permanent installation *Fallen Leaves* is housed in one of these 'voids'.

DANIEL LIBESKIND, **THE JEWISH MUSEUM, BERLIN,** 1989–98

'SOME PEOPLE TOLD ME THAT THIS [EXTERIOR CONSTRUCTION]
REMINDED THEM OF THE SAIL OF A BOAT.
ALTHOUGH I DO NOT CONTRADICT THIS STATEMENT, THIS IDEA PLAYED
NO PART WHEN I DESIGNED IT.'

Álvaro Siza Vieira

ÁLVARO SIZA VIEIRA, **PORTUGUESE PAVILION, EXPO '98, LISBON,** 1998

92

ÁLVARO SIZA VIEIRA
PORTUGUESE PAVILION, EXPO '98, LISBON

The motto for Expo '98, which took place in Lisbon from May to September 1998, reflected Portugal's seafaring tradition: 'The Oceans – A Heritage for the Future'. More than ten million people visited the Park of Nations, located a few kilometres north of the historic city centre. Along with the Vasco da Gama Tower and the Ponte Vasco da Gama, Europe's longest bridge, the Portuguese Pavilion was the fair's architectural highlight.

Álvaro Siza Vieira received the commission to build the Portuguese Pavilion in 1995. The brief was to create a main building that would be as flexible as possible for exhibitions and events of every kind. The intention was to convert the pavilion after the Expo for use by Portugal's Council of Ministers; it currently serves as a venue for temporary exhibitions. Siza was also commissioned to create an additional space for official events.

Most of the pavilions belonging to other nations were planned as tall buildings or were at least designed with 'towering hairstyles'. Siza therefore decided to make his a horizontal building that develops along the banks of the Tagus. A simple structure of exposed concrete was built around a central courtyard to accommodate exhibition rooms, a restaurant and the VIP rooms on the upper storey. The interior is flexibly structured so that it can be adapted to every possible use. The interior design of the exhibition rooms was created by Siza's colleague Eduardo Souto de Moura. Siza was responsible for all other design details, including the furniture, the drawings on the walls and even some of the crockery.

What makes the pavilion unique is the open area commissioned for official events, which abuts the building to the south. A thin concrete slab just 20 centimetres thick and 68 metres long spans the space between the two 14-metre-high end buildings without the aid of a single column. Its surface area measures more than 3,700 square metres. It is a strange feeling to look up at the curve in this large sail as one walks underneath it for the first time. It is reinforced with the steel wires by which it is also suspended from the end buildings. This creates a narrow gap through which light can enter. The interior walls of the end buildings are glazed with traditional ceramic tiles (*azulejos*) in Portugal's national colours of red and green.

With its impressively suspended canopy and elegant simplicity, the pavilion is virtually iconic. It comes as no surprise that in 2010 it was granted the protection of landmark status as a monument of public interest. Perhaps Álvaro Siza Vieira himself will one day be pronounced a national treasure as Portugal's most important architect.

ÁLVARO SIZA VIEIRA was born in 1933 in Matosinhos, near Porto. He studied architecture at the University of Porto, where he would later construct buildings for the Faculty of Architecture. The Boa Nova Tea House and the lido in Leça da Palmeira (1958–63) were his first independent buildings. Classic modernism is Siza's style, which he adapts as needed. He soon established a name for himself and began designing buildings on an international stage, including in Germany. In 1989 he was asked to plan the reconstruction of Lisbon's historic Chiado district, which had been badly damaged by fire the previous year. From 1993 to 1997 he designed and built an office building for himself and several colleagues. Siza has won many prestigious awards, including the Pritzker Prize (1992) and the Praemium Imperiale (1998).

'THE MOST MAGNIFICENT BUILDING OF OUR TIME'

Philip Johnson

FRANK GEHRY, **THE GUGGENHEIM MUSEUM, BILBAO,** 1993–97

93

FRANK GEHRY
GUGGENHEIM MUSEUM, BILBAO

With its spectacular museum for modern art, Bilbao catapulted itself in record time from a touristic no man's land onto the route of art and architecture pilgrims. Since the opening of Frank Gehry's Guggenheim Museum some ten million travellers have visited the Basque region's biggest city. This upgrading of a city through a prominent building has even been dubbed the 'Bilbao effect'.

And behind it all is the new building by Frank Gehry – a museum sculpture that lies stranded like a giant fish on the banks of the Nervión River in the city's former harbour district. Its gleaming scales change colour according to the time of day and are reflected in the water. Not just the façade but the entire museum seems to move in waves and curves, so that no one side of it resembles another. Gehry deconstructed the building into individual shapes that look as if they have been assembled at random. The main components of the stand-alone structure – completed in 1997 after a four-year construction period – are titanium and Spanish limestone. This combination of materials, as the architect noted, tests our conceptions of permanence: 'It is ironic that the stability of stone possesses only an apparent stability, because it disintegrates in the pollution of our cities, while titanium, which is just a third of a millimeter thick, provides a hundred-year guarantee against the air pollution in the city.' Titanium? Metallic surfaces are not unusual in Gehry's work, but the Guggenheim Museum in Bilbao is his first building covered in a titanium skin. The architect described his material of choice as being thin and yet curved like a cushion: 'It does not lie flat, and strong winds make it flutter.' In order to design the three-dimensional forms and their metal skin, the architect used a computer program that was originally developed for the space industry. The Basque outpost of the Guggenheim was the first large-scale design produced using this technology.

The essential – and intentional – dialogue between the stranded fish and its surroundings is ensured by glass curtain walls and a window-like opening along the river side. The sculptural building demands a great deal of attention in its own right, but it also affords spectacular space for art: among other exhibits, the museum scores with a vast space for Richard Serra's monumental *Ellipses* and his 172-tonne steel sculpture *Snake*. Gehry also wanted to use the 50-metre-high atrium as an exhibition space, but the clients persuaded him to allow the central area, which is bathed in light, to create its own special effect – as spectacular architecture.

FRANK GEHRY was born in Toronto in 1929 and has lived in Los Angeles since the age of 18. He studied architecture and town planning there and in Harvard. Since 1962 he has been designing projects in Europe, Asia and the United States together with his own firm – including private residences and museums, restaurants and libraries, concert halls, office buildings and shops. His buildings provide an exciting contrast between architecture and sculpture and often include new materials such as copper, zinc or – as in the Guggenheim Museum in Bilbao – titanium. Gehry has received numerous prizes and awards, including the Pritzker Prize, which he won in 1989.

94

SHIGERU BAN
JAPANESE PAVILION, EXPO 2000, HANOVER

One of the first projects realised by the young architect Shigeru Ban in 1986 was the design for an exhibition about his great role model, the Finnish architect Alvar Aalto (1898–1976). Aalto had incorporated a lot of wood into his work and Ban, too, wanted to use wood for his design. Since the budget did not stretch that far, Ban looked for an alternative and came up with the idea of using cardboard rolls instead.

This material became his trademark. Ban made a name for himself with his elegant villas and surprising constructions, but remained fascinated by cardboard rolls and continued to experiment with other recyclable materials. In 2000 he designed the Japanese Pavilion at the Hanover Expo, where the theme was 'Man – Nature – Technology'. The spectacular halls that Ban created out of cardboard rolls and paper won him international acclaim.

Using 440 cardboard rolls made of recycled paper, Ban designed a curved hall construction that was 16 metres high and covered 3,600 square metres of exhibition space. The cardboard rolls were up to 40 metres long and 12 centimetres in diameter. The joints were wrapped in plain adhesive tape, and the structure was covered with fireproof and waterproof paper. Unlike architects who build temporary exhibition structures that generally end up as industrial waste, Ban decided in favour of materials that could be recycled.

Shigeru Ban already had a good deal of experience in creating structures out of cardboard and board for humanitarian purposes. In 1994 he had begun to use these materials to build refugee shelters that were much more stable and more suitable than those being provided by the UN. He did this in response to the refugee crisis caused by the civil war in Rwanda. This was followed by provisional structures in other parts of the world: for victims of the 1995 earthquake that devasted the Japanese city of Kobe, where Ban also built a temporary church out of cardboard rolls; in India in 2001; in Sri Lanka after the tsunami of 2004; and in the Italian city of L'Aquila after the great earthquake of 2009. Ban's pro bono work also helped those left living in desperate conditions by the tsunami in Fukushima in 2011 and the earthquake in Haiti in 2012.

Shigeru Ban had long had misgivings about his profession. Architects usually design buildings for the rich and privileged: 'We are hired because the power of money is invisible. We are supposed to make power and money visible through monumental architecture.' For Ban, that is not enough, which is why time and again he uses his ideas and influence to help people in need.

Born in Tokyo in 1957, **SHIGERU BAN** studied in the USA. On his return to Tokyo he built private villas and commercial buildings before creating a sensation by using recyclable materials such as cardboard, paper and board. He also repurposed cargo or shipping containers into provisional buildings. When Ban won the commission to build the Centre Pompidou-Metz in the eastern French city of Metz, he used cardboard and paper to build his temporary office on the roof of the Centre Pompidou in Paris. For the roof construction of the museum, which was inaugurated in 2010, Ban drew his inspiration from a Chinese straw hat. In 2014 he was awarded the Pritzker Prize, in part for the development and construction of emergency shelters in crisis areas.

'PEOPLE DO NOT DIE FROM EARTHQUAKES. THEY DIE BECAUSE EARTHQUAKES CAUSE THEIR HOUSES TO COLLAPSE. THAT IS THE RESPONSIBILITY OF ARCHITECTS.'

Shigeru Ban

SHIGERU BAN, **JAPANESE PAVILION, EXPO 2000, HANOVER,** 2000

95

SANTIAGO CALATRAVA
AUDITORIO, SANTA CRUZ DE TENERIFE

The Spanish architect Santiago Calatrava's buildings are spectacular. From afar they look more like sculptures than buildings. The Valencian expresses the interplay of the two art forms as follows: 'Architecture and sculpture are two rivers in which the same water flows.' His fans often use the term 'archisculptures'.

Calatrava plays the part of both architect and engineer. After studying architecture, he felt the 'need to start again from the very beginning'. He took his motivation seriously and trained as an engineer. Since then the Spaniard has designed architectural forms in countless countries that were, until recently, unimaginable. One of these is to be found on the Canary Islands, on the island of Tenerife. In 1991 the administration commissioned the construction of the Auditorio, which houses a concert hall with approximately 1,500 seats and a chamber music room. The building, inaugurated in 2003, was built in the island's capital city, Santa Cruz. His spectacular concrete-shell roof is impressive even from a distance. The bent triangular shape curves over the rectangular building at a height of almost 60 metres. Viewed from the sea, it looks like another wave that is about to crash over the building, frozen at the moment when it crests. The arched concrete structures allow an interplay of light and shadow, and the illumination further emphasises the curved lines. The concert hall itself is located on a stepped base that contains the technical facilities. White wood panelling radiating outwards through the space creates excellent acoustics in the domed interior. Calatrava installed sound reflectors made of aluminium slats instead of stage curtains. The main hall is surmounted by a 50-metre-high dome that protrudes from the building in a pointed tip. Rows of windows built into the sides are reminiscent of human eyelids. The white tiles covering the dome and the building beneath provide a powerful colour contrast to the sea and the sky from every conceivable angle. Its proximity to the sea is not the only aspect that defines the island; the architect's use of local volcanic stone for the base of the structure also expresses its connection to the Canary Islands.

The commissioning body wanted a 'dynamic, monumental building that would be not only a space for music and culture, but also a symbol of the surroundings'. Mission accomplished!

SANTIAGO CALATRAVA was born in Benimàmet, near Valencia, in 1951. The Spaniard studied architecture in Valencia, followed by an engineering degree at the ETH Zurich, where in 1981 he also completed a PhD on the subject of 'the foldability of space frames'. His first office in Zurich was supplemented by branches in Paris and Valencia. Calatrava has developed numerous transportation hubs whose construction is transparent while revealing a sculptural effect. He often draws on organic forms such as insects, shells and leaves. His work has included numerous bridges, spectacular train stations, such as those in Zurich and Lyons, and many other architectural projects: from cultural and exhibition spaces to skyscrapers such as the Turning Torso in Malmö.

SANTIAGO CALATRAVA, **THE AUDITORIO, SANTA CRUZ DE TENERIFE,** 1991–2003

'PEOPLE OFTEN ASK ME WHETHER WOMEN WORK
DIFFERENTLY FROM MEN. ALL I CAN SAY IS THAT I DO NOT KNOW
AS I HAVE NEVER BEEN A MAN.'

Zaha Hadid

ZAHA HADID, **MAXXI – MUSEO NAZIONALE DELLE ARTI DEL XXI SECOLO, ROME,** 1998–2009

96

ZAHA HADID
MAXXI, ROME

The Guggenheim Museum in Bilbao (see page 236) caused a veritable boom: now every self-respecting city wants to build a modern museum that will revamp the city's image and boost tourism. Cities such as Paris, London and New York are less in need of these measures than medium-sized cities hoping to attract greater attention through the so-called 'Bilbao effect'.

Rome is by no means a medium-sized city, but when it comes to modern art, it has long been out of the loop. This changed when the Italian Ministry of Defence passed on to the Ministry of Culture the grounds on which a former barracks had stood. Its location is historically significant in architectural terms as it is located close to the famous Palazzetto dello Sport, built by Pier Luigi Nervi in 1960 and one of the last important modernist buildings to be constructed in Rome.

Rome's city fathers therefore decided that it was time to build a museum of modern art. Zaha Hadid's proposal narrowly beat the other competitors for the commission. What she then created fulfilled all expectations one might have of a modern museum in a classical city.

The National Museum of Arts of the 21st Century is the first public museum for contemporary art in Rome. In fact it consists of two museums, one for modern art, the other for contemporary architecture. This division into two – or rather, not the division, but the bringing together of the two parts – is simultaneously the underlying theme of the building. To reflect this, Zaha Hadid and her team created a complex formation consisting of various sections of the building, which flow together like rivers before separating again. It was important to her to create not a building but an ensemble that would 'nestle' into its surroundings with its intertwined forms. This led to the creation of a sort of campus that aims to be accessible to all and to dissolve the rigid boundaries between interior and exterior.

The idea of intermingling the individual segments becomes tangible inside the building. The various paths, bridges and other connections run through the entire museum as in a labyrinth, and connect the individual parts and the different levels in a unique way.

The recurrent criticism that new museum buildings do not serve art but overshadow it with their architecture – pressing the art up against the wall, so to speak – does not fluster Hadid. In her opinion, MAXXI is not a distraction but instead combines with the exhibited works of art to form a gesamtkunstwerk.

ZAHA HADID (born in Baghdad in 1950) is one of the few women to play a part in the circus of star architects working on the global stage. She began with a fire station, built in Weil am Rhein in 1993 for Vitra. Hadid had already had her own office since 1980 and had won a number of important architecture competitions, but until that point none of her designs had actually been built. She had, however, made a name for herself in the world of architecture with her designs and as an educator. It was only a matter of time before success came her way. She built the ski jump in Innsbruck in 1999–2002, and the Phaeno Science Centre in Wolfsburg in 2005. In 2004 Hadid became the first woman to be awarded the Pritzker Prize.

left Set in a neighbourhood whose buildings consist for the most part of former barracks and tenement buildings from the late 19th century, the MAXXI looks like a spaceship that is trying to remain undetected.

above Zaha Hadid plays with proportions so that visitors hardly realise how big the building really is. As with St Peter's Basilica, the true dimensions can be accurately gauged only when one sees a human being in front of the building.

ZAHA HADID, **MAXXI – MUSEO NAZIONALE DELLE ARTI DEL XXI SECOLO, ROME,** 1998–2009

'I SEE IN THIS COUNTRY GREAT TRANSFORMATIONS, GREAT CHANGES AND A GREAT CREATIVE POTENTIAL. AND I HAVE TO SAY THAT IN SOME WAYS THAT MEANS THAT THERE ARE FEWER CONSTRAINTS ON ONE'S WORK THAN IN THE WEST.'

Ole Scheeren

OLE SCHEEREN AND REM KOOLHAAS, **THE CHINA CENTRAL TELEVISION (CCTV) HEADQUARTERS, BEIJING,** 2002–13

97

OLE SCHEEREN AND REM KOOLHAAS
CHINA CENTRAL TELEVISON (CCTV) HEADQUARTERS, BEIJING

China's economic development has gathered breathtaking momentum. The shift from a planned economy to a market economy reached its pinnacle when China joined the World Trade Organisation in 2001. Throughout the country, factories and skyscrapers – and even entire cities – have sprung up overnight. Beijing is the centre of this development, and specifically the neighbourhood of Dongsanhuan, a business district in the east of the city.

This was the location chosen for the new headquarters of Chinese state television. The brief was to create space for news studios, the control room, programme production and the management, with offices for as many as 10,000 employees. The office of Rem Koolhaas, with a unique design by Ole Scheeren, won the protracted competition process.

The architects had thought about how to rise above the large number of sophisticated skyscrapers in the neighbourhood. The solution was hardly to build another, taller skyscraper. Ole Scheeren had the idea of creating a folded loop, or in his words: 'It is like a cage or a tube that is folded in space.' This tube is the second-largest office building in the world (after the Pentagon) and would, when unfolded vertically, be approximately 750 metres high.

The architects' clients were delighted, and yet they remained a little bit sceptical. Thirteen of the most experienced structural engineers in the country examined the plans for more than a year before the project was finally given the go-ahead. The result was a building that 'not only called into question the typology of the skyscraper, but also led to a radical redefinition of the fundamental characteristics of skyscrapers'. Above the base, which ranges from nine to 13 storeys, rise two towers that lean towards one another and that are connected at right angles for another nine to 13 storeys above the 36th storey (at a height of 160 metres). The most modern methods of computer analysis were needed to create this incomparable work. The main structure is an external steel skeleton with diagonal braces that distributes and channels the forces. These forces are reflected in the lattice pattern: the tighter the diagonal pattern, the greater the load.

Construction began in 2002. The external structure was completed in 2008 and work on the inside, including all studios, was finished in 2012. In 2013 the CCTV headquarters was voted the best skyscraper in the world by the Council on Tall Buildings and Urban Habitat (CTBUH) in Chicago. But is CCTV also the best television station? On this subject Ole Scheeren has said: 'There is a new generation at CCTV [...] They talk about role models such as the BBC and CNN.' Not everybody is convinced, however.

OLE SCHEEREN (born in Karlsruhe in 1971) is the young shooting star in the world of architecture. He began to work in his father's architectural firm at a young age and was just 31 years old when construction began on the CCTV headquarters. After his studies he worked in Rem Koolhaas's Office for Metropolitan Architecture (OMA) in Rotterdam in 1995. In 2002 he was made partner and in 2010 opened his own office. **REM KOOLHAAS** (born in Rotterdam in 1944) is one of the leading architects of our time. Aside from major international projects he also works as a theoretician and in this way has a profound influence on the Dutch and international architecture scenes.

98

HERZOG & DE MEURON
NATIONAL STADIUM, BEIJING

The Allianz Arena in Munich, the extension of Tate Modern in London, the Elbphilharmonie in Hamburg, the Sammlung Goetz in Munich and the National Stadium in Beijing appear to have little in common. They are not united by a shared style, the 'signature' for which so many artists and architects strive. It is, in a positive sense, 'style-less'. The link between these buildings lies in the architects who created them.

There are probably few architects who approach each project as an entirely blank slate in the same way that Jacques Herzog and Pierre de Meuron do. Even when the Swiss architects plan a stadium it bears no resemblance to the ones they have already built … apart from the fact that it is also a stadium. On the contrary: their style actually consists in making each of their buildings look entirely different from the rest.

Stadiums have a clearly defined function, and thus predetermined components. The sports grounds and the seats for the spectators are the most important parts. Herzog & de Meuron's structure for the National Stadium in Beijing is apparently chaotic, for it has no clearly visible hierarchical form and is open on all sides. It aims to invite people in. The association with a bird's nest spread rapidly, and so the stadium's nickname was born. This is no coincidence, however, as the Swiss architects study the conditions and culture of the various locations very closely. For the stadium in Beijing, they invited the Chinese artist Ai Weiwei to join their team as a 'cultural translator' to help them to avoid making any mistakes in this respect. 'The bird's-nest shape has a particular meaning in China. Birds' nests are delicacies in our restaurants and are considered to bestow good fortune,' as Ai Weiwei has explained. This made sense to the Chinese visitors at the Olympic Games in particular, and the stadium became a favourite with the public.

In terms of construction, the stadium consists of a concrete bowl with three tiers offering a total of 91,000 seats for spectators, encased in a steel construction weighing 42,500 tonnes. The thousands of different square hollow structural sections, which weigh up to 350 tonnes, were simply welded together like a 3D puzzle, without the need for screws and rivets. The bowl and the nest are in no way connected to one another because of the risk of earthquakes and the possible expansion of the steel if exposed to heat. The enormous sliding roof that had originally been planned for the stadium was not built in order to reduce costs – a decision that has certainly benefited the building. A transparent membrane to provide protection from the elements and improve acoustics was inserted between the strands of steel, in much the same way that birds used soft materials to seal the gaps between the twigs in their nests.

JACQUES HERZOG AND PIERRE DE MEURON (both born in Basel in 1950) have known each other since they were children. After completing their studies they opened a joint office in Basel in 1978. It continues to be the headquarters of their international architecture company, which employs more than 300 people. There are branch offices in London, Munich, Barcelona, San Francisco and Tokyo. Long regarded as an insider tip in architectural circles, the two men made their international breakthrough in 2000 with their design for the Tate Modern expansion. Before the Beijing commission, they had built the St. Jakob Park Stadium in Basel (2001) and the widely acclaimed Allianz Arena (2002–05) in Munich. Both men also teach at the universities of Zurich and Harvard.

'ALTHOUGH EVERYTHING ALWAYS SEEMS SO FINAL AND COMPLETED AT THE END, AT THE BEGINNING WE OFTEN DO NOT KNOW EXACTLY WHAT WE ARE DOING AND WHERE IT WILL LEAD US.'

Jacques Herzog

HERZOG & DE MEURON, **THE NATIONAL STADIUM, BEIJING,** 2003–08

99

ADRIAN SMITH
BURJ KHALIFA, DUBAI

When asked why they climb mountains, some mountaineers will say: 'Because they're there.' Some architects and engineers, if asked why they build ever higher buildings, will answer: 'Because it's possible. However interesting their motives may be, the question is, in the end, pointless as they will continue to carry out these activities regardless.

The technical challenges posed by a project such as the Burj Khalifa are, of course, extreme. The result – a spectacular view, newly created residential and office space and absolute exclusivity – is perhaps less important than the demonstration of the client's economic power. In this case the client was Dubai, or rather Mohammed bin Rashid Al Maktoum. Throughout the history of architecture the demonstration of power has always been an important motivation to construct a building in a particular way. Those who build skyscrapers are, in this respect, no different from those who once built churches, palaces and pyramids.

Even if the dimensions involved differed somewhat from everything that had gone before, the tallest building in the world was constructed using an almost classic technique – reinforced concrete with a curtain wall. The concrete was a new, special mixture. Given the high daytime temperatures in Dubai, it had to be pumped up at night, with cold water and ice added. In the light of such facts, the tower's proud claims to be ecologically sustainable are almost ironic, even cynical.

The aim was to exceed the 508 metres of the Taipei 101 tower in Taiwan. The original design aimed to add just ten metres to this, although no final decision about the height of the *burj* (the Arabic word for 'tower') had been taken when construction began. As the plans continued to develop, and construction progressed, the target height increased in several increments until it eventually reached 828 metres.

The building of skyscrapers on this level is a discipline all its own. It is impressive and fascinating, but the architect's signature becomes virtually invisible. In this particular case, the architect was Adrian Smith, who worked for the famous skyscraper office of Skidmore, Owings & Merrill in Chicago. The Guggenheim Museum in Bilbao, for example, is also a technical masterpiece, the difference being that the latter bears the traces of the architect and the architect's idea. In the case of extreme skyscrapers such as the Burj Khalifa, by contrast, the aim is different. As William Baker, the head engineer, put it: 'The Burj can be compared to a Lamborghini or a Ferrari: performance is the priority. And there is no such thing as more performance.'

The **TALLEST BUILDING IN THE WORLD** was actually supposed to be called Burj Dubai, but after the ruler of Abu Dhabi and president of the United Arab Emirates, Sheikh Khalifa bin Zayed Al Nahyan, leant a helping hand during a financial squeeze, it was named after him: Burj Khalifa. The tower is best described by superlatives: it is 828 metres high, has 160 floors, 57 lifts, the highest swimming pool, and consumes 946 cubic metres of water a day. As many as 12,000 people were involved in the construction of the building, at a cost of approximately 1.5 billion dollars. Some earned as little as 4 to 8 dollars per day, however. There has so far been one (official) suicide, by someone who leapt from the 147th floor – which is also a record.

'THE WORD 'IMPOSSIBLE' DOES NOT EXIST IN THE VOCABULARY OF LEADERS. NO MATTER HOW GREAT THE CHALLENGE, STRONG FAITH, RESOLUTION AND DETERMINATION WILL OVERCOME IT.'

Sheikh Mohammed bin Rashid Al Maktoum

ADRIAN SMITH, **THE BURJ KHALIFA, DUBAI**, 2004–10

'THE GREAT SPARKLING, THOROUGHLY STABLE SKYSCRAPER THAT
REACHES UP TOWARDS THE SKY NEXT TO THE MEMORIAL TO THOSE WHO WERE
MURDERED – THIS IS THE MIDDLE FINGER THAT AMERICA HOLDS UP TO
TERRORISTS AND THOSE WHO SYMPATHISE WITH THEM.'

Hannes Stein

DAVID CHILDS, **ONE WORLD TRADE CENTER, NEW YORK,** 2006–14

100

DAVID CHILDS
ONE WORLD TRADE CENTER, NEW YORK

Originally, the new tower in memory of the attacks on the World Trade Centre on 11 September 2001 was going to be called Freedom Tower. But at the signing of the first rental agreement with the Chinese industrial and banking corporation Vantone Industrial, commerce prevailed over commemoration and the tower was renamed One World Trade Center – because this makes it easir to rent out.

The architect is David Childs of Skidmore, Owings & Merrill, the same company that built the Burj Khalifa (see page 252). The tower does not stand alone, but within an ensemble of four other buildings that are part of the World Trade Center and the Ground Zero memorial site. The urban planning design was carried out by Daniel Libeskind, whose proposal won the architectural competition in 2002. The original design for the tower, too, was drawn up by Daniel Libeskind, though it underwent considerable changes by Childs. The square base goes up as far as the 20th floor. Above that, the design is that of a square into which a smaller square, turned by 45 degrees, has been embedded, so that the tower's floor-to-ceiling glass sides look like eight elongated triangles. One World Trade Center reaches the symbolic height of 1,776 feet (541.32 metres). It is therefore the tallest building in the USA and the fourth-tallest building in the world.

Although it is almost 300 metres smaller than the Burj Khalifa, the cost of building the tower – nearly 4 billion dollars – was more than double that of its 'colleague' in the desert. The reason for this is not only the difference in the workers' wages, but also the heightened security measures involved in the tower in New York. Childs wanted to build the safest skyscraper in the world. Unlike its two predecessors, it has a core of concrete that would not collapse under extreme heat, which is what the steel construction of the old towers did. The new tower was also constructed using a special kind of steel coated with an additional layer of fireproofing. After the foundation stone had been laid on 4 July 2004, the 20-tonne foundation stone was dug up again and repositioned because it was decided that the tower should be built at least eight metres back from the road to guard against car-bomb attacks. A special kind of concrete at the building's core, steel beams encased in concrete, bulletproof glass and an entrance hall 20 metres high and enveloped in concrete walls make One World Trade Center a bunker in the shape of a skyscraper. Additional architectural measures are in place in case of an attack: wider staircases and filter systems that offer protection in the event of a chemical or biological attack, and there are even light strips on the ground.

The place where the **TWIN TOWERS** once stood is now the site of a memorial, whose construction began in 2006. The plans for the memorial were also drawn up by Daniel Libeskind, and were later developed and executed in cooperation with Michael Arad and Peter Walker. Like footprints marking the position and size (almost one hectare each) of the destroyed towers, two pools nine metres deep have been built into the ground of the enormous piece of land amid more than 400 trees planted there. They are the biggest artificial waterfalls in the USA. Encircling the pools are copper plates inscribed with the names of the 2,983 victims of the attacks in 2001 and 1993. The memorial was opened on 12 September 2011.

GLOSSARY

Art Deco

A decorative style of the 1920s and 1930s, characterised by elegant but simple forms (in contrast to the linear richness of Art Nouveau), bold colours and the use of precious materials such as lacquer, ivory, marble, chrome, etc. It was named after an exhibition of applied arts held in Paris in 1925.

Art Nouveau

Around 1900, when science and technology were developing rapidly, many architects, sculptors and painters, as well as carpenters, glaziers and jewellers, looked back to the traditional craftsmanship of past centuries. They were passionate about sweeping lines and decorative ornaments. The movement had different names in different countries: Jugendstil, Art Nouveau or Modernism. The appearance of Barcelona was transformed by Antoní Gaudí, Lluis Domènech i Montaner, and others. They integrated a great variety of stylistic quotations into their residential buildings, parks and public buildings, and used mosaics, glazed ceramics and other craft techniques to created colourful, asymmetrical designs strongly influenced by nature, and in particular by plant forms.

Baroque

The Baroque period was the age of political absolutism and, therefore, of the conspicuous display of power, opulence and wealth. The secular and religious worlds were closely linked; the splendour of the churches and monasteries in Europe is in no way different from that of the palaces. The architectural design, all interior decor, and often even the landscape in which the building was set were elements of the Baroque 'total work of art'. Stretching from around 1600 to the middle of the 18th century, the Baroque style developed throughout Europe, though often with clear national differences. The decorative but much lighter style known as Rococo emerged from late Baroque during the 18th century.

Basilica

(Greek *stoá basiliké*: 'king's hall') In antiquity, a grand, hall-like public building consisting of a long central section (nave) flanked by two aisles that are separated from the nave by rows of columns. The nave is wider and considerably higher than the two side aisles. The basilica became one of the most important forms of early Christian and mediaeval church building. In its church form, an altar niche (the apse) is usually attached to the east end of the nave.

Choir

The altar area at the east end of a church, originally reserved for the clergy. Initially separated from the rest of the church by a chancel screen, over time it developed its own distinctive architectural form and decoration (such as choir stalls). Among its special features are the ambulatory (an extension of the side aisles around the choir) and choir chapels.

Column

A perpendicular building support (of wood, stone or metal) with a round cross-section – this distinguishes it from half-columns, pillars and pilasters. In contrast to a pillar, a column does not necessarily play a structural role: it can be merely decorative. Columns can also be free-standing monuments: a well-known example is Nelson's Column in London. A column's structure and decoration are based on the three main classical forms: Doric, Ionic and Corinthian.

Cornice

A decorative moulding designed to mark the transitions between the horizontal sections of a building. They are typically found on an entablature, a wall (usually high up), the point where a wall and roof meet, over a window or door, and on a pedestal.

Frieze

Initially part of the entablature in Greek temple, a frieze later became a long, horizontal band on a wall, internal or external, carrying painted or carved ornaments or figural representations. Architecturally, a frieze serves to articulate a large expanse of wall.

Gothic

Around the middle of the 12th century, something new developed out of the heavy forms of Romanesque architecture. Cathedrals became higher, round arches became pointed, ceilings were constructed of arched vaults supported by slender ribs, and externally, buttresses were used to support the walls. These basic structural elements created a strong framework that carried the weight of the building. Now freed from this task, the walls could be pierced by windows, flooding the interior with brightly coloured light. The Gothic style, which originated in France, soon spread to England, Germany, the Netherlands, Spain and Italy, and in one form or another endured until about 1500.

International Style

During the 1930s and 1940s, many buildings were characterised by simple geometrical forms, such as white cubes, arranged asymmetrically, with windows set in horizontal bands. In 1932, Philip C. Johnson and Henry-Russell Hitchcock devoted an exhibition, *The International Style: Architecture Since 1922*, to this style. The proponents of this movement focused on the functional, and largely ignored the decorative aspects of design. This style is clearly seen in the buildings of Mies van der Rohe, who is generally considered to be the father of the International Style. It spread from the United States to South America, Europe and Asia – it was indeed international. Other important representatives of the style were Walter Gropius and Le Corbusier.

Loggia

(Italian: 'columned hall') A part of a building open on at least one side, which, in contrast to the portico or balcony, does not protrude beyond the building's profile. The open sides are often supported by slender columns. Loggias were particularly popular in the palaces of the Italian Renaissance.

Neo-Classicism

A style in art and architecture, flourishing c. 1770–1840, that was a reaction to the light, playful, organic forms of the Rococo period. Based on a return to the architecture of classical antiquity, it employed characteristic elements of Greek and Roman design, notably columns, pediments and porticos. The emphasis was on order, proportion, a restrained grandeur and a sometimes austere simplicity. By the middle of the 18th century, Italy – and Rome in particular – had become the source of inspiration for artists, architects, writers and political thinkers. The Brandenburg Gate in Berlin, the Arc-de-Triomphe in Paris, the British Museum in London, and the Capitol in Washington, DC, are among the most famous Neo-Classical buildings.

Obelisk

(Latin *obeliscus*, Greek *obelískos*: 'pointed column') A four-sided, tapering stone column in the form of a very slender pyramid, used as a solitarily standing monument.

Orangerie

Originally, an exotic collection of citrus trees at European courts in the 16th century. In time, the term was used of the buildings or rooms used to protect the trees. Often elegantly designed, these were frequently used for social events.

Palace Construction

See page 108

Pantheon

(Greek *pan*: 'all' and *theós*: 'god') In ancient Greece, a sanctuary dedicated to 'all the gods'. Over time, this meaning expanded and today the term is generally used of a monument honouring a country's illustrious dead. The oldest preserved building of this kind is the Pantheon in Rome, which was erected under Emperor Hadrian in the 2nd century AD.

Plan centré

See page 31

Pylon

In ancient Egyptian architecture, a heavy, tapering tower forming part of the monumental gate leading to a temple complex. In modern architecture, pylons are either supporting or framing structures intended to absorb compressive forces (e.g. the pylons carrying electricity cables).

Relief

A sculpture in which the forms project from a flat surface (of stone, wood, metal or ivory). Reliefs were often used to decorate the surfaces of buildings, such as the walls (internal and external), pediments and church portals. They were particularly popular in ancient Greece and Rome, and also Renaissance Italy.

Renaissance

See pages 93, 94

Romanesque

See pages 53, 57

Skyscrapers

Initially, skyscrapers were built mainly in Chicago in the aftermath of the Great Fire of 1871, and at first they were called 'cloud scrapers'. What made their unheard-of height possible was the use of steel frames; walls no longer had to support the building, and so they could be covered in huge areas of glass. Buildings were now so tall, lifts had to be used rather than stairways. The basic design changed little over the years.

The fashion for the skyscraper soon made its way from Chicago to New York, which was soon completely transformed by them. Originally, they were office buildings, but by the 1930s they were also being built as apartment blocks. The development of skyscrapers was encouraged by a desire to erect the world's highest building, a title long held by the Empire State Building in New York.

Spolia

(Latin *spolium*: 'booty, something taken from the enemy') Building elements plundered from older buildings (especially those of antiquity) in order to be reused in a later building. Typically columns, sculptures, friezes, capitals, architraves, lintels etc. Originally, old buildings were exploited simply because they provided an inexpensive source of building material. In time, however, the cultural references made by the spolia became increasingly important.

Stupa

(Sanskrit *stup*: 'pile up, accumulate') Originally, a round mound of earth built up over a grave. Within a few centuries, this simple burial mound developed into the basic form of the classical Buddhist stupa: a square platform on which sits a hemispheric dome surmounted by a crown and spire. The oldest construction of this kind, found in Sanchi in Central India, was built in the 3rd century BC.

Tracery

The ornate stone ribbing in the windows of Gothic churches. Its basic purpose is structural – it supports large areas of glass – but it also has an important decorative function. It developed during the High Gothic era in France and reached its peak in the English Perpendicular Style.

Transept

In a church, one of the short 'arms' that intersects the nave at the east end, near the altar, usually aligned north-south.

PHOTO CREDITS

akg-images: 21 (Jochen Helle); 24/25, 79 (Manuel Cohen); 48 (James Morris); 56 (Alfons Rath); 65, 132, 151 (Bildarchiv Monheim); 70 (JBE Photo); 71 (De Agostini Picture Lib./C. Sappa); 76, 77 (VIEW Pictures/James Brittain); 87 (Hilbich); 92, 97, 100 (Rabatti-Domingie); 95 (ANA); 102, 161 (Schütze/Rodemann); 107 (Pirozzi); 110 (Yvan Travert); 124 (De Agostini Picture Lib./G. P. Cavallero); 133 (Bildarchiv Steffens); 146, 175; 156 (Doris Poklekowski); 168/169 (Gerard Degeorge); 227 (Jürgen Raible); Anthony Oliver, London: 165; bpk: 143 (Hans Christian Krass); getty images: 63 (Eye Ubiquitous), 220/221; 223 (View Pictures); 246 (Bloomberg); 252 (Ozgur Donmaz); laif: 8 (Francis Leroy/hemis.fr); 11; 13 (Rene Mattes/hemis.fr); 15, 158 (Bertrand Gardel/hemis.fr); 16 (Dagmar Schwelle); 18 (Domenico Tondini/hemis.fr); 23; 242; 152/153 (Dorothea Schmid); 26 (Arnaud Chicurel/hemis.fr); 28 (Michael Turek/Gallery Stock); 29 (Frank Heuer); 30, 32, 33 (Markus Kirchgessner); 35 (Franck Guiziou/hemis.fr); 36, 90 (Martin/Le Figaro Magazine); 38 (Jacques Gillardi/hemis.fr); 43 (Marc-Oliver Schulz); 41, 46, 203, 206/207 (Hemispheres); 42, 122/123, 121 (Bertrand Rieger/hemis.fr); 44, 47 (Tobias Hauser); 51, 214 (Jan-Peter Boening/Agentur Zenit); 52 (Graeme Peacock/Arcaid); 55 (Colin Dixon/Arcaid); 58 (Glyn Thomas/Loop Images); 60 (Richard Soberka/hemis.fr); 66; 68 (Martin Westlake/Gallery Stock); 73 (Hal Beral/VWPics/Redux); 75 (RABOUAN Jean-Baptiste/hemis.fr); 80/81 (Sylvain Sonnet/hemis.fr); 82 (Frank Tophoven); 84/85 (Marc-Oliver Schulz); 89 (Joerg Modrow); 98 (Plambeck); 104, 144, 205, 229 (Frank Heuer); 105 (David Clapp/Arcaid); 109; 112 (Zoratti/Ambience/Arcaid); 114 (Katharina Hesse); 116 (Rene Mattes/hemis.fr); 117 (Billon/ChinaFotoPress); 119 (Bruno Morandi); 126, 129, 134 (Pierre Adenis/GAFF); 130 (Ralf Brunner); 138 (James O. Davies/Arcaid); 140; 149, 178 (Hollandse Hoogte); 155; 158 (Bertrand Gardel/hemis.fr); 163 (Sasse); 166 (Yann Doelan/hemis.fr); 170 (Berthold Steinhilber); 173 (Bernd Jonkmanns); 175 (Sergi Reboredo/VWPics/Redux); 177 (Marc-Oliver Schulz); 180 (Michael Danner); 183 (Toma Babovic); 184, 185 (VU); 187 (David Clapp/Arcaid); 190, 198 (Christian Heeb); 193; 197 (Justin Merriman The New York Times/NYT/Redux); 200 (Joshua Lutz/Redux); 208 (Matthew Worsnick/Arcaid); 211 (Galit Seligmann/Arcaid); 212 (Henning Bock); 216 (Bungert); 219 (Michael Riehle); 224 (Arnaud Chicurel/hemis.fr); 230, 232 (Pierre Adenis); 233 (Pierre-Olivier Deschamps/VU); 234 (Amin Akhtar); 236 (Miquel Gonzalez); 241 (Burg + Schuh/Palladium); 244 (Antonello Nusca/Polaris); 245 (Michele Palazzi); 249 (Paul Spierenburg); 251; Mark Lyon: 188; mauritius images/Alamy: 239; Saline royale: 137; Matz und Schenk/Dombauhütte Köln: 148

IMPRINT

© Prestel Verlag, Munich · London · New York, 2015
© for the works reproduced is held by the architects, their heirs or assigns, with the exception of: Alvar Aalto, Santiago Calatrava, Walter Gropius, Gerrit Rietveld, Hans Scharoun, Ludwig Mies van der Rohe, Frank Lloyd Wright with © VG Bild-Kunst, Bonn 2014; Louise Bourgeois with © The Easton Foundation/VG Bild-Kunst, Bonn 2014; Le Corbusier with © FLC/VG Bild-Kunst, Bonn 2014; Shigeru Ban with © Shigeru Ban Architects; Günter Behnisch with © BEHNISCH ARCHITEKTEN, Stuttgart; David Childs with © Skidmore, Owings & Merrill LLP; Frank Gehry with © Gehry Partners, LLP; Zaha Hadid with © Zaha Hadid Architects; Herzog & de Meuron with © Herzog & de Meuron; Louis Kahn with © Architectural Archives of the University of Pennsylvania; Daniel Libeskind with © Studio Daniel Libeskind; Oscar Niemeyer with © Oscar Niemeyer Foundation; I.M.Pei with © Pyramide du Louvre, arch. I.M.Pei, Musée du Louvre; Renzo Piano and Richard Rogers with © Renzo Piano Building Workshop and Rogers Stirk Harbour + Partners LLP; Gerhard Richter with © Gerhard Richter, Köln; Alvaro Siza Vieira with © AlvaroSizaVieira.com 2014

Front cover (from left to right): *Pantheon*, Rome, see p. 22; Frank Gehry, *Guggenheim Museum*, Bilbao, see p. 236; *Great Temple*, Abu Simbel, see p. 10; Jørn Utzon, *Opera House*, Sydney, see p. 222; *Taj Mahal*, Agra, see p. 118; Gustave Eiffel, *Eiffel Tower*, Paris, see p. 158; Westminster Abbey, London, see p. 74; Oscar Niemeyer, *National Congress and Cathedral,* Brasília, see p. 210; George Bähr, *Frauenkirche*, Dresden, see p. 128; William Van Alen, *Chrysler Building*, New York, see p. 190; *Cathedral of Santa Maria Del Fiore*, Florence, see p. 94; *Colosseum*, Rome, see p. 20
Back cover (from top to bottom): *Borobudur*, Java, (detail), see p. 46; *Santa Maria Assunta and Campanile*, Pisa, see p. 60; *Hagia Sophia*, Istanbul, see p. 26; *Westminster Abbey*, London, see p. 74; *Guggenheim Museum*, New York, see pp. 206/07
Frontispiece: *Taj Mahal*, Agra, India, see p. 118
Page 6: Frank Gehry, *Guggenheim Museum*, Bilbao, see p. 236

Texts by (numbers refer to chapter numbers):
Isabel Kuhl: 1, 4, 6, 7, 9, 10, 11, 13, 14, 15, 18, 25, 26, 27, 29, 30, 31, 32, 34, 36, 37, 38, 40, 41, 42, 43, 44, 45, 46, 47, 53, 55, 57, 59, 60, 62, 64, 68, 71, 74, 76, 78, 79, 80, 82, 86, 87, 91, 93, 95
Florian Heine: 2, 3, 5, 8, 12, 16, 17, 19, 20, 21, 22, 23, 24, 28, 33, 35, 39, 48, 49, 50, 51, 52, 54, 56, 58, 61, 63, 65, 66, 67, 69, 70, 72, 73, 75, 77, 81, 83, 84, 85, 88, 89, 90, 92, 94, 96, 97, 98, 99, 100

Prestel Verlag, Munich
A member of Verlagsgruppe
Random House GmbH
Neumarkter Strasse 28
81673 Munich
Phone +49 (0)89 4136-0
Fax +49 (0)89 4136-2335
www.prestel.de

Prestel Publishing Ltd.
14-17 Wells Street
London W1T 3PD
Phone +44 (0)20 7323 5004
Fax +44 (0)20 7323 0271
www.prestel.com

Prestel Publishing
900 Broadway, Suite 603
New York, NY 10003
Phone 212-995-2720 ext 22
Fax 212-995-2733
www.prestel.com

Library of Congress Control Number: 2014960122; British Library Cataloguing-in-Publication Data: a catalogue record for this book is available from the British Library; Deutsche Nationalbibliothek holds a record of this publication in the Deutsche Nationalbibliografie; detailed bibliographical data can be found under: http://www.dnb.de

Prestel books are available worldwide. Please contact your nearest bookseller or one of the above addresses for information concerning your local distributor.

Translated from the German by: Jane Michael, Munich
Copy-edited by: Danko Szabó, Munich
Editorial direction: Julie Kiefer
Project management: Dorothea Bethke
Picture editor: Dorothea Bethke
Cover and design: Wolfram Söll
Layout: Wolfram Söll
Production: Astrid Wedemeyer
Origination: ReproLine Mediateam, Munich
Printing and Binding: Print Consult GmbH, Munich

MIX
Paper from
responsible sources
FSC® C084279
www.fsc.org

Verlagsgruppe Random House FSC®-N001967
The FSC®-certified paper Profibulk was supplied by Igepa.

ISBN 978-3-7913-8126-8